BULLETPROOF

Lauraine E. White

LIMITS OF LIABILITY AND DISCLAIMER OF WARRANTY

The author and publisher shall not be liable for your misuse of this material. This book is strictly for informational and educational purposes.

WARNING – DISCLAIMER

The purpose of this book is to educate and entertain. The author and/or publisher do not guarantee that anyone following these techniques, suggestions, tips, ideas, or strategies will become successful. The author and/or publisher shall have neither liability nor responsibility to anyone with respect to any loss or damage caused, or alleged to be caused, directly or indirectly by the information contained in this book.

Cover Design by: Veezie Forbes Design Studio, Atlanta, GA
Interior design and formatting by KUHN Design Group | kuhndesigngroup.com
Photography by: Gerren K. Clark and Neiko James of Chris Perfect Studios
Editing Consultant: Michelle Shelfer

Lauraine E. White
laurainewhite@gmail.com
www.miracle-movement.com

PREFACE

t was a beautiful Saturday afternoon in August. The park was filled with spectators, walkers, pet play times, and lovers of music and art. It was our first date. Love was in the air.

Fast forward twenty years, and the love waned. Love no longer lived here. What happened?

Love is some kind of animal. It's either a pet or a beast. One you embrace, and the other makes you fearful of coming close to it. But love was meant to enhance our lives. We just can't have the love we desire without understanding the part the One who is Love must play in helping us realize how to get it.

If you consider love a game where there are winners and losers, you don't understand. Love is a journey, and we have the power to create what it looks and feels like. We are the drivers of that vehicle that will bring our life's fulfillment.

I thank God for this journey. He is the source of this writing, and I rode His Holy Spirit like on eagle's wings to accomplish its completion.

When I wanted to give up, He gave me the courage to keep going—to fight to stay above water and get the sustenance that I needed to keep all the balls flowing in the air as I juggled, navigating this writing voyage.

If you've resolved that your present circumstance is all life has to offer, I'm here to challenge you. There is more available to you, but you have to participate. You've got to work for it.

Anything worth having is worth fighting for. That includes your life. Your destiny is calling you higher. Come and take this journey with us. We're excited about your future.

CONTENTS

CONTENTS

1

SHOOTERS

The weapons we fight with are not the weapons of the world. On the contrary, they have divine power to demolish strongholds. We demolish arguments and every pretension that sets itself up against the knowledge of God, and we take captive every thought to make it obedient to Christ. And we will be ready to punish every act of disobedience, once your obedience is complete.

2 CORINTHIANS 10:4–6 NIV

I'm sitting in the driver's seat of a car in a business district of a town that I'm not familiar with. I'm not sure where I am or whose car it is that I'm sitting in, but I'm apparently waiting for someone.

I'm patiently waiting but concerned. I begin to look in the rear- and side-view mirrors as if I'm expecting someone to show up at any time along the thoroughfare—but they don't. So, I keep waiting.

What? Are those gunshots that I hear in the distance? This appears to be a safe area of town, and I don't feel any immediate alarm about any of it, but why are they shooting in broad daylight?

The sound of the gunshots grows louder, but I don't drive off. I continue to sit there, waiting with a strange feeling in my gut. I slide down in the driver's seat of the car until I am lying face down on the seat.

The sound grows louder, and I notice a gunman approaching the car that I am in. At that moment, my thoughts are racing a mile a minute. I need to remain as still as possible—motionless so that he goes away assuming that I am dead.

But he approaches the car anyway, unloading ammunition from his high-powered automatic weapon into the car that I'm in. Then a second, third, and fourth gunman join him. All of a sudden, the car is completely surrounded by gunmen, shooting to kill.

It seems as if the shooting will never end. They continue shooting for what seems to be forever as I wait motionless. As I'm lying on my face, I feel the impact and smell the fumes from the smoke that rises from the ricocheting bullets penetrating the metal frame of the car. There's smoke everywhere.

Suddenly, the gunshots stop. One by one, the gunmen leave the area. I'm still lying face down in the front driver's seat, but I can see the faces of people as they come up to the car, looking in and walking away crying.

They think that I'm dead. I even see my ex-husband walk over to the car, look in, and begin crying.

They all believe that I am dead. The realization of what's happening causes me to muster the nerve to sit up in the car to see what's happening and to let them know that I'm okay—I'm alive—but no one pays attention to me. No one seems to care. I appear invisible to them, or I really am dead.

As I rise up, I notice white wing feathers that are blowing in the wind outside the window of the car. I get out without opening the car door, and although the air is still filled with smoke outside, I see

the most amazing sight. The car that I've been in is completely surrounded by angels. They don't look at me, move, or say anything.
They remain positioned around the car, one angel's wing overlapping
the other until the entire car is wrapped with angels—even the roof,
windshield, and bumper are covered. Their eyes are fixed straight
ahead, and they don't move to say a word. They are there performing God's Word.

"Bulletproof" is what I hear as I wake up...

I sit on the side of my bed, shaken by this dream. It's October 4,
2016—the feast day of Rosh Hashanah. What does it mean? What's
the message in it for me?

**The car that I've been in is completely surrounded by
angels. They don't look at me, move, or say anything.**

I realize that there's a lot of imagery in this dream and there are
many meanings that can be derived from it, but I'm painfully aware
that God has a specific lesson that He needs you and me to take
away from it.

Starting with the car, I believe there are two areas that it represents. They are:

- My life
- The Church, universally

If this is the case, I'm sure there are many of you that say, "How
can this be? You're not the Church." But I am the Church. Whether
as a single individual or as a group, we are all individually the Church
just as much as we are collectively.

What I do every day represents God, whether it's good or bad that I choose to do. When I lie, I'm representing God, and when I tell the truth, I'm representing God, and He's not sorry that He made the offer to me to be His ambassador in the first place. My choice to do good or evil doesn't lessen His commitment to His original offer, nor does it negate my responsibility to represent Him well.

I don't have the opportunity to put on and take off my life in Christ at will. I know this may not sit well with some people, but it's true.

When I chose to accept God's offer of salvation, my life changed. I looked the same. I did a lot of the same things, but every day with Him, there are small and minor changes that took place in me—up to and including today.

I was still a liar, but I lied less. How is this possible? Because the Holy Spirit became my friend—not my prosecutor, nor judge and jury, as many of us were taught. In fact, as life became entrenched with pain and misery and I was faced with difficult choices, He became my best friend. He's now my constant confidante.

We're all looking for a friend that won't sell us out—a friend that sticks close when times get tough. When money is low and friends are few, but when you're God's friend, He uses His spiritual PayPal to send appropriate resources to support you.

A friend that tells you the truth about a situation is what we're all looking for. You know. A true friend tells you what other people don't have the nerve to tell you out of fear of what your response will be or out of their own hidden agendas. There are no hidden agendas with God.

When everyone around me was gone, whether through death or desertion, I placed more and more importance on my relationship with God because it was the only relationship that was reliable. He won't die and leave me because He's eternal. He also won't desert me when life becomes too much to bear or when someone better comes along.

So back to my original point—in this dream, the car represents my life and the life of the Church. What's significant about this fact?

I'm waiting. The car is not moving. I won't drive off because I'm waiting for something or someone.

What or who am I waiting on? Who or what is the Church waiting for? That's the question. I believe that the two—individual believers and the Church as a whole—work hand in hand.

For me, I realize that this car represents my life from 2001 to 2013. I was too afraid to sit up in "the car" to witness God's protective shield because I didn't know it was safe to do so. I was lying on my face, praying and fasting but not confident of the safety that God promised and provided. I was clueless.

My ignorance never prevented God from protecting me, though. He did it anyway.

I was waiting for life to get better. I started out early in life with the promise of and passion for being a singer. Those dreams fell flat when I left school and realized everyone has talent. It's drive, zeal, and tenacity that won't give up when you hear *no* after *no* and that moves the mountains of the music and entertainment industries. Life happened, and I had to make a living instead. So, pursuing my music career had to wait.

There's that word again. Wait.

I was waiting on God to fix everything—my broken life, my family, my job, and my money issues. I had so many broken dreams and unfulfilled promises that they could fill a lifetime of oceans.

I was waiting for God to give me answers to all of my problems. I found out it doesn't work that way. God is not a genie in a bottle. You can't rub the bottle a little and the genie pops out to grant you three wishes. No. It's through working out problems that you find solutions.

My mother was a mathematician. She loved to work on long, difficult math problems. It excited her. You could see the joy in her face when the question mark showed on your face as you tried to work the problem.

Many times, I wanted to try to take a shortcut to find the answer, but she would scold me, saying, "You can't shortchange the process. You've got to show all of the work. Work the steps, and they'll work for you," she would say.

It's the same with life's dilemmas. We would all love to avoid struggling to solve problems in life, but we can't. We can't hide from them. We can't throw money at them to fix them.

You have to do the work. There's just no way around it. Trying to go around problems only leads to brick walls, and those aren't for you to climb over. You have to take a hammer to them and bust through. You can't even hire workers to do the work for you.

I've met so many people that hire coaches to help them work through difficulties, but there are issues with this. Many of these coaches haven't worked through their own problems. How is it that someone who can't work through their own obstacles can help you solve yours?

Some haven't lived long enough to have gone through anything similar to what you're paying them to help solve. The prescribed formulas don't work for every situation. When you're in a tough place, you need someone who's been *through* where you're trying to get through.

My biggest problem was me. I kept getting in the way of the apparent solutions that were glaring in front of me. During those times, I just couldn't see them.

Why wasn't I *bold* enough to drive the car? I thought I was waiting on other people. I thought I was waiting on God, but everything I needed was already there. Why couldn't I see that? I was caught up in the physical, but God transcends the physical.

There's a weight that comes from waiting. Not just a heaviness that builds in your spirit while waiting but the weight that's gained from just sitting. You become sedentary, complacent, and disillusioned during the wait until you are almost like someone who is sedated. You're numb.

How did you get here? You don't know what to do or how to proceed through the mess and mire of life's painful choices.

Every one of us suffers in some way or another. No one gets away without some pain. It's what you do with the pain that's key to making life work.

The last ten years were very hard and trying for me, but I persevered through them, with the help of the Lord. I had to get up and show up every day, whether I felt like it or not. Many times, I felt like giving up, but God wouldn't let me. The Holy Spirit pushed me to actively participate in the process so that the outcomes overshadowed the obstacles.

Looking back over the years, I realize that in many instances and through many periods of time, I just merely went through the motions of living. I worked. I ate. I played, but I didn't do what I thought I was born to do.

All of this represents the reasons I was waiting. What are the reasons for the Church waiting?

During the same ten or more years, we've seen the Church suffer, too. At the hands of greedy and vicious leaders of individual church congregations, we have witnessed memberships dwindle down and

many churches forced to close. At the height of the economic down-
turn, banks foreclosed on churches across the nation at alarming numbers because they weren't able to pay their bills.

According to churchtrac.com, "pre-pandemic, approximately
3,500 people left the religious congregations every day. That's a rate
of 1.2 million walking away from church every year…. However, on
average, churches are at 85% of their pre-pandemic attendance level."[1]

I know people who sit on their couch or at their desk Sunday
after Sunday, watching the Word on a screen instead of going to
worship because they became disenfranchised by the system of the
church. They didn't give up on God. They gave up on church. They
still love God. They just can't stomach going to church anymore. It
is too much work.

It is worse than going to work. There is a whole lot of back-bit-
ing, stabbing each other in the back, and fighting over who will be
in charge. Like crabs trying to get out of the bucket, everyone's vying
for position. Whether it's the deacon board, the mother's board—
even who's going to lead prayer on Sunday morning—divisiveness
leads to arguments and disgruntled assemblies of the castaways that
weren't chosen to be out front.

It's called offense and comes from the spirit of Leviathan. Everything done sets something off. Anything they do causes you to
become offended. This spirit rips apart families and churches, causing irreparable damage that goes on for generations. It's what caused
Cain to hate his brother, Abel. It caused an annihilation of Job's life.
It wreaks havoc and blows down everything in its way. It kills the
cause of Christ.

1. "The State of Church Attendance: Trends and Statistics (2023)," *ChurchTrac Blog*, 2023, churchtrac.com/articles/the-state-of-church-attendance-trends-and-statistics-2023.

If you couldn't lead, you left. This made those who left get the bright idea to start their own church.

Of course, what begins in chaos ends in chaos. You can't begin a thing with the wrong intent and expect it to turn out well. Confusion begets more confusion. Hostility births out more hostility.

You can't breed something that you are not. Your children will look and act just like you. If you can't follow, how could you believe that you would attract those who will follow you?

Utterly insane and chaotic assemblies of misfits and outcasts are what we had—all across the nation. This led to a mass exodus of those upset by being overlooked, underutilized, broken, hurt, and wounded by misled and overly zealous wannabe leaders who were sent to do just what they did—destroy the original intent of what the Church is to be.

Was this what Christ had in mind when He said, "I will build My Church; and the gates of hell shall not prevail against it"? I don't think so. This represents hell coming against the Church and the Church hiding in caves instead of standing up against such foolishness.

And I'm to blame for all of this because just as I said before, I am the Church. No blame can be cast without casting guilt on me in all of this, too.

I watched and participated, too. Where were the courageous followers of Christ? Just as I slid down in the driver's seat of the car in my dream, so was the Church lurking in parked cars instead of boldly putting our feet on the pedals and driving.

The other important factor about this dream is that it happens on Rosh Hashanah, which is the Jewish New Year. It marks the beginning of humanity through the creation of Adam and Eve. It's celebrated with the blowing of the shofar and begins ten days of repentance that peak on Yom Kippur, the Day of Atonement.

Why is this important? God is the one who established Rosh Hashanah and Yom Kippur to coincide with the fall agricultural cycle. According to Leviticus 23:24–25, God told the children of Israel through Moses that on the first day of the seventh month, they are to observe total rest by not working and to commemorate this sacred occasion with loud horn blasts.

This solemn occasion is thought to be a time of judgment that can be averted during the ten days of awe that happen between Rosh Hashanah and Yom Kippur, which is a day when they can obtain atonement for their sins.

The Church is the Bride of Christ, yet we don't celebrate any of our husband's family traditions. Why is that the case? I know that Jesus is the fulfillment of this festival, but should we not observe it, knowing that we had no chance of salvation without its existence?

What's this notion of complete rest? In Matthew 11:28–30, Jesus says of himself, "Come to Me, all who are weary and burdened, and I will give you rest. Take My yoke upon you and learn from Me, for I am gentle and humble in heart, and you will find rest for your souls. For My yoke is comfortable, and My burden is light." Jesus bears witness of Himself as the fulfillment of this festival that calls for rest. We rest in Him, knowing that the day we repent, He forgives us.

You may ask—what's significant about these festivals in light of this notion of being "bulletproof"? After God created the world and placed Adam and Eve in the garden, they disobeyed God by eating the fruit of the tree of the knowledge of good and evil. As soon as they ate it, they realized they were naked. Prior to this, they had no sense of there being anything wrong with their nakedness.

Their eyes were opened to a new reality. They sensed that by hiding their nakedness, they could also hide from God. You can hide from people, but you cannot hide from God. God knew they were hiding and came looking for them.

"Where are you?" God asked. He knew where they were but asked the question as a discourse with man. God consistently deals with us. What He did before, He's doing now.

Today, God's asking the same questions of us. Where are you? Why are you hiding? He is calling us back to our first love, which is Jesus—not for religion's sake but for a relationship with Him.

He's giving us another chance—a do-over. He wants introspection from us. Repentance and remorse are the keys for us to move ahead. We need to reflect on how good and merciful God is. This knowledge should cause us to fall on our knees with reverence because we don't deserve so great a salvation.

Once we know better, we do better. Armed with this knowledge, we can confidently drive the Lord's Church to where He's leading us, and resting in Jesus as our shield, we can be bulletproof.

2

ARMED AND DANGEROUS

How do you fight an invisible enemy?

While serving at a remote village in Africa, a missionary and his wife journeyed through the jungle to Addis Ababa, Ethiopia, for supplies every other week. It took two days to get there, which meant they had to set up camp overnight.

On one of those trips, they arrived in the city but needed cash to purchase medicine and supplies before heading back to the hospital. So, they stopped at an ATM.

Once they arrived, the missionary noticed two men fighting, and one was seriously injured. They stopped to treat the injured man and at the same time talked to him about the Lord.

They then traveled for two days, camping overnight, and arrived home without incident. Two weeks later, they made the trip again.

When they arrived, they saw the young man that had been injured. He told them that he knew they got money out of the ATM and that they had medicine because he watched them from the moment they entered the city. He said, "My friends and I followed you into the jungle, hoping for a chance to attack you. We planned to kill both of you and then take your money and drugs. But just as we were about to attack, we saw that you were surrounded by thirty-three armed men."

The missionary laughed and said, "It was just the two of us at that campsite."

"No, sir, and I wasn't the only one to see those guards. My friends saw them, too. In fact, we counted them. It was because of those guards that we left you alone."

A year went by, and the missionary and his wife returned to the States to visit family. He was invited to speak at the local congregation that sent them to Ethiopia and told this story during his message. Once he mentioned the armed men, a man interrupted him, asking if he remembered the day it happened. The missionary gave the date, and the man who interrupted told him this story:

"On the night of your incident in Africa, it was morning here, and I was on my way to go play golf, but I felt the urge to pray for you. In fact, it was so strong, I called men from this church to meet with me here in the sanctuary to pray for you. Would all of those men who prayed with me on that day stand up?"

The men who met together to pray that day stood up. With extreme excitement, the missionary counted them. There were thirty-three![2]

This compelling story reminds us that our prayers make a difference. It points to the truth that God will move heaven and earth when we pray. There are so many stories of God answering prayers.

Here's another one. I found an article about a fourteen-year-old young man named John Smith from Missouri who was dead for forty-five minutes. A common name, but he experienced an uncommon miracle.

---

2. Source unknown.

He spent fifteen minutes submerged in an icy lake in February 2015, and doctors performed CPR for twenty-seven minutes trying to revive him, to no avail. When his mother came into the hospital room, she began to pray, loudly asking God to send His Holy Spirit to save her son. And God answered, because the moment that she finished her request, suddenly the doctor got a pulse reading from John.

The entire hospital staff, emergency technicians, and all of John's friends got to witness God's supernatural power at work because of a mother's prayer.[3]

Let's face it, most people don't want to turn on the news out of fear of what new disaster has taken place, who's shot whom, and so forth and so on. They also cringe when they hear that governments are enacting laws that go against God's perfect plan for living. Whether Christian or not, most people agree that some of the things that the world accepts now are just foolish.

We are also seeing an increase in natural disasters that are rocking the planet. Instead of seeing the correlation between a world gone mad and these phenomena, people write it off as climate change. No. It's God trying to get us to change.

The problem is that on many of the issues that are directly against God's Word, the Church is silent. In some instances, we are conflicted on what is right. We are at odds with each other on where we stand regarding hot political topics, and the world is watching us as we are in constant disagreement about what God's Word *really* says about any given issue.

---

3. Erik Ortiz, "Missouri Teen Submerged in Icy Lake for 15 Minutes Makes 'Miracle' Recovery," NBC News, February 5, 2015, nbcnews.com/news/us-news/missouri-teen-submerged-icy-lake-15-minutes -makes-miracle-recovery-n300841.

Instead of rising up as one body of believers in defense of what our faith is built on, we shy away from anything that makes us look like we're intolerant of change. So, we sit in our pews silently.

We have church conferences and fellowships, and we love to sing, dance, and shout, but when the party is over, many go home to miserable circumstances. What did we accomplish?

If I want to party, I'll go to a party, but when I need God to show me how to live with power—how to fight for what's mine—I don't need a party or a good fellowship. I need to be equipped. I need to know how to fight.

What we have now, as the saga of navigating this life continues to turn, is a sedated Church. We're numb. At best, we're a sleeping giant without the power that's been given to us by our resurrected Savior.

I don't need a party or a good fellowship. I need to be equipped. I need to know how to fight.

It's a sad commentary when the same people go to church every Sunday and come home the same way. They're miserable. They're sick with all types of diseases even though Christ specifically took thirty-nine stripes so that all thirty-nine classifications of disease could be eradicated for the believer. If only we would believe this truth. We wouldn't have so many living hopeless lives. They believe in the hope the doctor gives through the dispensing of medications, but those same medications are what keep them sick. Don't get me wrong—I believe all knowledge is given by God, and that includes medical knowledge.

When all hell breaks loose against your home, you need to know how to enlist all of heaven to work on your behalf, not just call on someone to pray for you. You don't need to talk about your problems. You need solutions. You need to tell those who brought the problems in the first place—and it's not people but principalities—to get off of your property.

I've spoken at churches that have been in existence for hundreds of years, but they don't even have a prayer ministry. Hello? What's wrong with this picture?

Jesus said in Matthew 21:13, "'My house will be called a house of prayer'; but you are making it a den of robbers." What happened? Why did we stop praying as the universal Body? It's obvious that this has been a consistent issue from the beginning of time—that God has to step in and herd His people back to Him—because Jesus was actually quoting prophecies from Isaiah and Jeremiah.

Yes, there will always be individuals who pray, because God always has those who will not bow to another, but I'm speaking of the collective group of believers that are the *ecclesia*—those called out by God to serve Him.

There's a saying that's been used for centuries: "If you want peace, then prepare for war." War is not the absence of peace. War is peace. In other words, peace is predicated on how well you are prepared for and equipped for the battle. Therefore, war causes peace to exist.

In case you didn't know, you are in a battle. I believe you will be in any one of these given states of being at all times: you're either in a battle, you're just leaving one, or you're headed into one. The key is being equipped. You need strategies to overcome the devices of your enemy.

The struggle is real. Many times, warriors get weary fighting the same enemy because this enemy doesn't grow tired, and he uses our own strategies against us.

That means to be armed and dangerous, we must first become broken. It's in the breaking of our will that God's will can be done. That's a weapon.

Psalm 51:17 says, "A broken and a contrite heart, God, You will not despise." The breaking prepares the heart to hear God's message.

Has your heart ever been broken? Mine has, and after going through it, you never see things quite the same. That's called transformation. God uses a crushed life to change the world.

"He was crushed for our wrongdoings; the punishment for our well-being was laid upon Him, and by His wounds we are healed" (Isaiah 53:5). The crushing of our Lord and Savior changed the world because it was so undeserved. The piercing and wrenching toil the Master endured all for love's sake causes us to want to change.

It's not until you and I are bruised by life's challenges that we understand. This transformation makes the heart ripe for God to pick.

Another weapon we have in our arsenal is praise. I know you've probably heard the saying, "Just praise your way through," but the praise that is a weapon isn't fake. It comes from a genuine heart.

I know. You may be in a place where you can't see a reason to praise God. All you feel that you can give is conjured-up praise. I get it. Life has been rude, hard, and brash. From where you sit, there's been no sign of a Savior. How do you find genuine praise for an unknown, unseen God?

Faith comes by hearing. Have you heard what Jesus has done? When there's little evidence of what He's personally done for you, praise Him for what He's done for others. Praise Him for healing the lame man. Praise Him for saving the woman at the well, who had been married multiple times and felt that all she was now worthy of was to accept just living with a man who had no commitment to her.

Praise and adore Him for raising Lazarus from the dead. Then you can praise Him for raising your dead life to live eternally with Him.

That's the power given to us by God through His written Word. It establishes a testimony in us before we have our own. That's why the Bible is also a weapon of mass destruction.

Satan's goal is to render us powerless by silencing our testimony. But our testimony is what causes us to overcome. That's why we can't be silent.

At the name of Jesus, demons tremble, so call out His Name. It moves mountains. "The name of the LORD is a strong tower; the righteous runs into it and is safe" (Proverbs 18:10). His name is not just a safe haven. It's a weapon.

At the mention of His name, heaven stands at attention. "And it shall be that everyone who calls on the name of the Lord will be saved" (Acts 2:21). He is King of all kings and Lord of all lords.

We must know who Jesus is and be able to defend what we believe about Him. Jesus wanted to know what people were saying about Him. He asked His disciples, "Who do people say that the Son of Man is?" (Matthew 16:13). Most people thought of Him as a prophet—some said John the Baptist and others said Elijah or Jeremiah. Then Jesus asked, "But who do you yourselves say that I am?" (Matthew 16:15). That's when Peter made the boldest statement of all, and that is that Jesus is the Christ, the Son of the living God. At that confession, Jesus laid down His plans for His Church. He said, "I will give you the keys of the kingdom of heaven; and whatever you bind on earth shall have been bound in heaven, and whatever you loose on earth shall have been loosed in heaven" (Matthew 16:19).

What's this notion of binding and loosing? Binding has several meanings, but I believe that this Scripture is in reference to agreements.

In an agreement, there are stipulations that cause it to be binding. That type of binding is what causes it to be legally unavoidable and such that it cannot be undone or stopped.

That means if you bind anything in prayer that aligns with God's will, it becomes legally binding in heaven. That takes away power from Satan when we exercise this right. No one else but heaven has to agree with you, but the Word says that if two agree on anything on earth, it will be done for them.

That means there's more legal binding in heaven when two people on earth pray in agreement. That's why the spirit of Leviathan works so hard to keep us at odds with each other—because he understands the power of our agreement. When we agree, heaven sees our unity under the blood and gives us access to the throne room of heaven. That's a key to our freedom.

In my dream, while I appear to be waiting on God, He's waiting for me to put "the key" that He's given me in the ignition and drive. The keys that Jesus mentions in Matthew 16:19 are the missing link to our freedom.

Just dangling the keys won't give us power. It's the key put in the ignition and turning the car on that gives us power—the power to move mountains. Jesus said that what we release on earth is released in heaven. That means at the moment we ask, heaven answers.

But what if heaven's answer is no? A no signifies that our request is not aligned with God's original plan. That's the reason that when we accept Jesus as our Savior, we also need to receive the Holy Spirit.

The Holy Spirit will lead you to all truth, including what to pray for. The Holy Spirit, a type of down payment of sorts to our heavenly home, comes to complete the work of salvation in us. We're not holy, but He is. He wants to become our constant companion to help us live our new life, thereby sealing the promise. He convicts us so that we have a change of heart regarding sin.

Understanding the order of things is one of the keys that helps to unlock the kingdom of heaven. We can't unlock the kingdom while being carnal. We must "put on" holiness like a garment. Starting out, we need to be very intentional with it until it becomes a part of who we are.

Why did Jesus, before He left earth, instruct His disciples not to leave Jerusalem but to wait for the Holy Spirit? There's something to be said about obedience.

You must remember that after Jesus was crucified, buried, and risen, the disciples were in hiding. They were scared. The Pharisees, Sadducees, and other officials were making up stories about the removal of the stone and Jesus's missing body. They even paid off the guards who were hired to stand watch in order for them to corroborate the pack of lies that they fed the public.

The disciples of Jesus were shaking in their boots with fear of being killed too. They were hiding. Then Jesus showed up. They touched Him and felt where He was pierced in the side. He was alive.

For forty days after His death, Jesus presented Himself to His disciples as evidence that He, in fact, was who He said He was. But things were happening so fast.

All of a sudden, Jesus was lifted from the ground. They watched as a cloud took Him up until they saw Him no more. Can you imagine being there—watching the one you looked to for everything over the past three years—and now He was gone? What devastation they must've felt.

Yet, Jesus told them to stay right in the center of the hot seat, Jerusalem. It was the central business district for all things religious and was the very thing they were hiding from. They wanted to run away from that place. But at Jesus's convincing demonstration of His deity, they were moved to obedience. After watching Jesus ascend into heaven, who wouldn't obey even at the threat of being killed?

Secondly, they were ten days away from Shavuot, or Pentecost, which is fifty days after Passover. During those fifty days, Jews count the Omer. This involves the practice of counting down the days from Passover to Pentecost (Shavuot). This is significant since Passover is the historical marking of the Hebrews leaving Egypt, and Shavuot is considered the establishment of God's covenant with the chosen people through the giving of the Ten Commandments. There are fifty days between the two feasts.

The Passover (exodus out of Egypt) also marks the time of Jesus's crucifixion, and Shavuot (giving of the Ten Commandments), or Pentecost, is the beginning of Christ's Church. God is consistent, and Jesus is the fulfillment of every Jewish feast and festival. The coinciding of these events is evidence of God's providence.

So, the disciples were waiting. More than one hundred and twenty people were gathered together, waiting. Then the day came, and suddenly a violent noise, like that of a mighty wind, filled the house where they were. Tongues of fire sat above each of the one hundred and twenty, and everything changed. The world hasn't been the same since Christ's Church was ushered in and the Holy Spirit became the powerhouse of fuel for it.

It started with obedience. They obeyed Jesus. They did what was contrary to what was instinctive. Out of fear, they wanted to be anywhere other than Jerusalem. But the promise would only come to them in Jerusalem.

They had to face their fears, overcoming the obstacles that stood in the way of receiving their promise. That's a lesson for us today.

Don't allow anything to stand between you and the promises of God. Fear robs us and tells us what we already know is better than what we don't know. But we don't know what we don't know. That's why we need the Holy Spirit. He tells the truth.

We don't fight as the world fights. This spiritual fight is only possible when we put on the full armor of God so that we are equipped to fight for our destinies. This armor is not as many have purported because we don't fully understand how to make this happen, and even when we do, it takes divine strategies to maneuver through spiritual battles. But the fight is fixed. Therefore, in order to win, we fix our eyes on the One who fixed it. In Ephesians 6:13–18 it says,

> Therefore, take up the full armor of God, so that you will be able to resist on the evil day, and having done everything, to stand firm. Stand firm therefore, having belted your waist with truth, and having put on the breastplate of righteousness, and having strapped on your feet the preparation of the Gospel of peace; in addition to all, taking up the shield of faith with which you will be able to extinguish all the flaming arrows of the evil one. And take the helmet of salvation and the sword of the Spirit, which is the Word of God.

So, here's the list of the armor that we need:

1. Belt of Truth
2. Breastplate of Righteousness
3. Shoes of the Gospel of Peace
4. Shield of Faith
5. Helmet of Salvation
6. Sword of the Spirit

We will deal with each of these individually to give depth to our understanding. The first—the Belt of Truth.

This isn't related to the belt that you use to hold up your pants. It's more like a tool belt where a craftsman keeps his tools while working. This refers to the belt of a soldier. It's where he stores his weapons while on the battlefield. He needs them close so that they are readily available when he needs them. He doesn't need to scramble around trying to figure out where a certain weapon is when he needs it. He needs to know exactly where it is—especially in the heat of battle.

Why is it called the Belt of Truth, and why do you start there? You must know the truth, for the truth is what sets you free. The truth is that Jesus is the promised Messiah—that He is the Christ, the Son of the living God. The truth that you must have, sharpened like a weapon, is that Jesus is our Lord and Savior.

Why start there? It's because that truth is the foundation of who we are and why we do what we do.

The second piece of armor is the Breastplate of Righteousness. The breastplate of a soldier covers the most vital organs of a man. It is made of steel and is solid. Nothing can penetrate it—not even a sword.

Why righteousness? Don't you remember that Jesus said that there are none righteous? How can this be accomplished?

It happens through the finished work of the cross. This righteousness that we put on is not based on what we do but because of what Jesus has done for us. It's a gift from God. It was packaged by the unselfish acts of our Savior and sealed by His blood.

Now we come to number three—Shoes of the Gospel of Peace. We would never wear high-heeled shoes on a battlefield, right? The shoes for a soldier must be tough and able to handle any terrain. That means maybe steel-toe boots with thick soles. They have to hold up in any weather.

Why the Gospel of Peace for our feet? Our feet carry us wherever we go. The shoes symbolize the foundation on which we stand—the Gospel. The message that we carry must be one of peace.

There's another piece on this idea of peace. When we are in spiritual warfare, it's easy to become worn down when we fight from the place of our flesh.

The good news in this war is that your enemy is already defeated. Having a foundation built on that Gospel should bring peace—not turmoil or restlessness. Don't become weary and don't allow anything to rattle you. It's important to stay at peace through the rocky seasons of warfare. Rest in that peace while you are living—not just after you transition from this life.

That's why we need to understand our position when we pray. When we petition heaven, we do it from the place where Jesus is seated—at the right hand of the Father. Remember this is only possible because "those who worship Him must worship in spirit and truth" (John 4:24). We transcend this physical body when we enter into His gates with praise and thanksgiving while praying. Our worship ushers us into God's presence. It brings us into the throne room of heaven, where we have access to the Father. It's no ordinary thing. It's supernatural. That's good news.

The fourth piece of armor is the Shield of Faith. The shield is an important piece in our garment. I find it interesting that it requires faith.

"Now faith is the substance of things hoped for, the evidence of things not seen" (Hebrews 11:1 KJV). This armor is tangible and built up over time. Our stamina and endurance are built up by putting the armor on every day. This faith is put on like a garment, and we never take it off. The more we wear it, the more we realize how important it is.

Where does it come from and how do we exercise it? Faith starts and ends with God but is introduced through others or through trials and tribulations. Either way, God orchestrates the outcome. Notice that I said the outcome and not the messes that we endure. He's the problem solver, not the creator of our problems. His desire is for our good.

Jesus said that if we have faith the size of a mustard seed, we can speak to the mountains in our lives, and they will be moved. Mountains, whether literal or figurative, are large and overwhelming. The idea that all we need is a smidgeon of faith when we pray and God will move the impossible for us is inconceivable. It's tough to fathom that all things are now possible.

That's what this piece of armor feels like. It's lightweight because God is the one doing the heavy lifting.

"Without faith it is impossible to please God" (Hebrews 11:6 NIV). Pleasing God takes faith and comes by taking life one day at a time. But once you've tasted how good He is, you want more.

That's how it must've been with Abraham. Consider that God began to speak to Abraham while he was still worshipping idols— yes—Abraham came from a family of idol worshippers. He wasn't seeking God. God was seeking him.

It's the same with you and me. God seeks to have a relationship with us. He puts an ounce or so of faith in us—even in the atheist—so that He has the opportunity to kindle it if we open that door to Him.

The fifth piece of armor is the Helmet of Salvation. The brain is the *central intelligence agency* for the warrior in the army of God. If your opponent pierces through your helmet, it's over. Therefore, protective gear for the head is essential, and the idea that salvation is the protector of it is significant.

It's also essential that the helmet has openings for us to see through. We don't need to blindly follow. God wants us to be fully aware, and that means we need to see what's ahead.

That's the role that the Holy Spirit plays. He helps us navigate the battle, giving us insight on strategies to overcome.

The warfare that we are engaged in is against an egotistical and arrogant foe. He hates the idea that God loves us and chooses to have a relationship with us. It makes his blood boil. That's why he never stops his attempts at defeating us.

He was once God's favorite. God used to love him like that, and he's jealous of us. Are you getting a clear picture of why he's so vengeful?

That's why we're in a war against Satan. The place of the battle is in our minds. He takes our thoughts captive, putting them behind prison walls, telling us who we are not, and that God doesn't exist. If we believe that God exists, he'll try to convince us that He doesn't love us—that we're unworthy of God's love.

Salvation has to be the helmet. You've got to know that you know that you know: Jesus is alive, and He saved you. You need to know that like you know your name. Never waiver. It's a weapon as well as your gear. A soldier that's unsure in using his weapon is a danger to himself and to the rest of the soldiers. You must know with assurance that you are loved and your salvation is secure.

The sixth and final piece of armor is the Sword of the Spirit, which is the Word of God. The word *sword* has "word" in it, which is key to understanding its power.

It's a weapon. It's "sharper than any twoedged sword, piercing even to the dividing asunder of soul and spirit, and of the joints and marrow, and is a discerner of the thoughts and intents of the heart" (Hebrews 4:12–13 KJV). The Word gets through when nothing else will. In Jeremiah 1, Jeremiah gives the account of God calling him as His prophet. As God interacts with Jeremiah early on, He asks him what he sees. After Jeremiah responds, God tells him that He is "watching over My Word to perform it" (Jeremiah 1:12). That's powerful.

Make no mistake about it, praying the Word moves God. It demonstrates your allegiance to Him that first, you know His Word—whether you just looked it up today because it's relevant to your circumstances or you memorized it years ago—and secondly, that you are bringing Him into remembrance of it.

That's why the Bible has been strategically laid out as it has been—so that every circumstance has a piece of the Word that we can stand firm on when the enemy comes to destroy our arguments.

Get in the Word. Study it. When you do, pray and ask the Holy Spirit to lead you. When you're unsure, google what you need by asking for a Scripture reference for it. It works.

These strategies are tools for equipping and preparing you for God's army so that you become weapons of mass destruction against the army of darkness. Put on your armor so that you effectively stand firm against the wiles of Satan as he roams the earth looking for someone to devour.

3

TWELVE

*The City shimmered like a precious gem, light-filled,
pulsing light. She had a wall majestic and high with
twelve gates. At each gate stood an Angel, and on the
gates were inscribed the names of the Twelve Tribes of
the sons of Israel: three gates on the east, three gates on
the north, three gates on the south, three gates on the
west. The wall was set on twelve foundations, the names
of the Twelve Apostles of the Lamb inscribed on them.*

REVELATION 21:12–14 MSG

Twelve. One and two side by side. There are twelve tribes of Israel.
God promised that twelve princes would come from Ishmael
(Genesis 17:20; 25:16). Twelve spies were sent to spy out the
promised land (Numbers 13; Deuteronomy 1:23). Twelve stones were
to be taken from the Jordan River to serve as a memorial that God
had dried up the Jordan so that the ark of the covenant and the people could cross it (Joshua 4:1–9, 20). Elisha was plowing with twelve
yoke of oxen when Elijah called him (1 Kings 19:19).

There were twelve gates that had twelve angels at the great, high wall
that represented the twelve tribes of Israel, and there was a promise that
the twelve apostles will have a say in who enters the "pearly gates" from

the house of Israel (Revelation 21:12; Matthew 19:28). Jesus was twelve years old when He questioned scholars in the temple (Luke 2:41–52).

Did you know that Abraham's firstborn son, Ishmael, had twelve sons? They became the twelve tribal rulers of their settlements (Genesis 25:16).

Even the heavens are impacted by the number twelve because the stars pass through twelve zodiac signs in their heavenly processional, which also coincide with the twelve months, both in our Gregorian and in Jewish calendars. Many Christians won't address this because they've been told that this is worldly—not of God. But there's significance in its details because we do believe the Word that says, "In the beginning God created the heavens and the earth." If we believe that Word, then this truth of the heavens is significant.

It's in the details that God works. He doesn't leave anything out, and nothing is left to chance. You may or may not agree or believe this to be true—that God prominently utilizes numbers to impact our systems. But it's not in our beliefs that this becomes true; it is the truth because God is.

There's no denying it. The number twelve is a prominent number referenced in the Bible by God, not man. In fact, the number twelve is mentioned one hundred and eighty-seven times. In Biblical numerology, twelve means government, and when God wants to infuse into the world's system of government, He uses twelve people to impact the entire world.

God notably used twelve men—we call them apostles—to build and establish His Church after validating everything that He had promised them. He proved who He is through performing the ultimate miracle. He got up out of the grave. It's empty. Instead of decaying bones, ashes, or any other evidence of death, He came back to life so that we know that He did it.

The point is that God is intentional in His choice of numbers. With intention, He allowed Jacob, the trickster, to have exactly twelve sons, and He determined before time began that out of these sons, He would create the nation from which the Savior would be born.

All of those crooked, murderous, scheming, adulterous, and of-ill-repute relatives are the people that God chose for His Son, who never did any wrong, to be raised and nurtured by. They looked and acted a lot like us.

Everything had to line up just right for Jesus to enter the world. Even their wickedness had to play out so that God could use righteous men to write laws—corrective measures to move us from wrong to right and to demonstrate who He is.

On the day that I began writing this chapter, Billy Graham, at ninety-nine years old, transitioned from this life into eternity. Before the day began, I asked Holy Spirit, "Why on earth is it significant for me to write this chapter today?" Little did I know that Billy Graham would transition on that day, but God knew, and He positioned me to have a reason to write with passion and resolve about what's important to Him concerning His Church.

Billy Graham was important to God's plans. He lived on purpose and demonstrated what it means to lose your life in order to find it.

Bishop Milton Perry was my father in ministry, and I loved him dearly. He spoke fondly many times about how Billy Graham was on the cutting edge of ministry. He spoke of how he was the first white minister of the Gospel to fully embrace him, being an African American preacher, during the '50s. That was a time when the separation of races, not just in society but also in the Church, was highly sensitive, and an aggressive act such as this could've killed his influence. Billy Graham did it anyway.

I believe this is what Jesus is looking for as He reroutes His Church. Cutting-edge leadership that won't back down in the face of adversity is what He needs now. He doesn't need those that will go along to get along—or to get a loan.

He's looking for those that will sell out their lives to choose His life— a life that means you've got to carry a cross, not run from it. Or you may be assigned to help bear someone else's as they carry their own cross.

I believe Billy Graham's death is significant in God's timetable for a mighty move with signs and wonders for the world to know who He is. This is a "parting-of-the-Red-Sea" moment in history, and we get to participate with God as He performs it.

This move of God will test what you know and believe about Him, though. A part of this move includes the same sign that Jesus pronounced for the age that He walked this earth. That sign is the sign of Jonah and not as you suppose.

Jonah needed to repent—not just Nineveh. Yes, Jonah had good reason to hate the people of Nineveh. They had a well-known history of tormenting the Israelites. This harassment may have even hit Jonah's hometown in such a way that his anger burned against them.

He wanted justice. He wanted God to punish them for what they did against his people Israel. Just as we sometimes do.

Can you feel Jonah's pain? Maybe you still have some doubt about his hesitancy in preaching repentance to the people of Nineveh. I understand. There are details that aren't fully explained because those for whom the book of Jonah was written knew the fine points all too well.

Let me explain it this way. Compare the people of Nineveh to Hitler and Germany between 1919 until Hitler's death in 1945 when

World War II ended. Roughly six million Jews were slaughtered under his reign of terror as he took over one European country after another.

There was blood of innocent people who committed no crime in his wind and all over his hands. He brutalized them and separated families. He put them in concentration camps and tormented them for the thrill of it.

Imagine that. The people of Nineveh were guilty of these types of crimes against the children of Israel. That's why Jonah hated them so much and tried to demand justice from God. Justified punishment is what Jonah was seeking from the only one that he knew could hurt them where it mattered—God.

Jonah was pushing the envelope with God, though, because he knew all too well about God's unfailing love and mercy and couldn't fathom God changing His mind about them. How could He? I mean, they were atrocious in their treatment of the children of Israel. How dare He forgive them, right?

So, Jonah decided to leave town instead. This had to be better than watching God forgive them once they repented. It seemed logical to him.

Haven't you felt that way before? I have. I can name people that I once hated. Death wouldn't have been too much of a punishment for them from my point of view, but that wasn't what God had in mind. He wanted me to forgive them instead.

It's confession time. I once hated white people. It wasn't known in public. I was a closet hater of white people. You know, I only discussed my disdain for them around other people who hated white people, too. That wasn't just black people that I talked to either.

When I was at school, at work, or had to sing at white churches or other white establishments, I appeared to love them. Isn't that what "good Christians" do? You pretend. You lie to others and to yourself. I was a good liar, or so I thought. I had on my game face in all public places, but in private my hatred boiled against them—just like Jonah's did against the people of Nineveh.

They could die for all I cared. It was justifiable. They always got promotions without being qualified for them. They got preference when I was standing in line for help from a merchant unless the other customer's conscience wouldn't allow this to happen, and they would call the salesperson on the carpet for their actions.

They would even follow me around the store—watching me, as if I came to steal from that store. You know—"all black people steal." So, they watched me. They didn't try to hide what they were doing, either. They did it openly. They were proud to protect what they perceived to be theirs.

But I can go deeper—just like I did on Jonah's account. There's slavery. My people were ripped from their native countries and brought to this nation across one of the largest bodies of water, stripping my people of paths and patterns known to them and giving them no chance of escaping to return to their native lands—all for their selfish reasons. They wanted to control us.

They enslaved us. They put us in chains. Not just chains on our extremities but also in our minds. That's how they dominated us. They changed our names as a way of controlling our mental capacity to orchestrate a breakout from their tyranny, manipulating our future for generations.

They had plans to annihilate us if we tried to escape. That is, until they realized that if they killed us, they were destroying their money source. You see, killing us during slavery was like burning money in a pit. Apart from how they got rich was that after paying handsomely to purchase slaves, the government allowed them to place a dollar value—stating what they were worth—on each slave's head on the plantation. Wealth creation and the slave owners' freedom from taxation were more important than the freedom of black people.

Oh yeah, I had a reason to hate. Off the backs of my people, they got rich. Empires were created from the sweat of the brows of my ancestors. Even what we call the White House was built, maintained, and sheltered by my abused and mistreated relatives.

When my grandfather got to work that morning, he found out that his son was hung in the bathroom. You talk about humiliation. That's shameful.

Yes, I have cause to hate. I can bring it home for you, too. My mother's brother was hung by white people. He was killed at work—right in Birmingham, Alabama.

He found out that there were men that worked side by side with him, doing the exact same work that he did, but who got paid a whole lot more than anyone else. He complained about it to one of the supervisors although my grandfather, who worked at this same company, warned him not to because of what they might do. He did it anyway.

They were "moonshining," as they called it. The business had a side hustle where they made moonshine and sold it for handsome returns on their investment. These guys that delivered the products on behalf of the company were paid more than double what was paid to the other workers for their additional services.

One day, the supervisor asked my uncle to come to work early because they had a special assignment for him, too. Unsuspecting of their contrived arrangements, my uncle went along with them and came into work earlier than normal.

When my grandfather got to work that morning, he found out that his son was hung in the bathroom. You talk about humiliation. That's shameful. My grandfather continued to work for that company—for people that murdered his son. He worked side by side with men that took the life of his son until they closed the doors of the company during the depression. These men never went to prison for the crimes committed against our family.

Oh yeah, I have reasons to hate white people. But God... He manipulated my life in such a way, through hardships and painful sets of experiences—because He loves me—that I got to see life from His view.

On purpose, God made me preach on Jonah. As I do every time that I'm asked to speak before God's people, I studied the backstory. God was manipulating my understanding through this exercise that He knows all too well that I practice.

Because God's Spirit lives in me, He broke me down—from within my spirit—to orchestrate the change in me that He wanted. Through this same story of Jonah, it was as if He placed a mirror in front of me to make me take a long, hard look at myself as I dug deeper to understand why Jonah did what he did.

He began with me. He wanted me to see what my hatred did to me. My hatred hurt me, not those I hated. My intention was to hurt them, as crazy as that sounds now, by hating them, but I was so wrong. I was destroying my potential through my hatred. They didn't even recognize that I hated them. Many times, I don't think they cared. It wasn't even an afterthought for them. But it consumed me—day and night. God began the clean-out process with me and not them.

My hatred was like a disease. It was ugly. It was grotesque. Just like cancer spreads when untreated, this active hatred overtook all my emotions, and even with my game face on, I was only deceiving me. Every encounter gripped my soul and wouldn't let go. But those nagging episodes increasingly ate away at my potential for change to occur. It appeared that the more I faked, the more I had to be around white people.

It's like what you don't want to happen, happens. Almost as if your psyche takes over your reality, causing what you don't want to come into existence to show up. The more I tried to deceive, the more I got let down, and the angst that grew within me overpowered my sense of worth.

"For as a man thinks in his heart, so is he" (see Proverbs 23:7) says it best. I was fooling myself. My reality became my worst nightmare. I let it get the best of me but couldn't let go of the dangling rope that was connecting me to this nonsense because I couldn't "see."

The opposing idea of what "they" think about black people was becoming true for me. And I knew this wasn't what I wanted at all. This made life unbearable, but I didn't know that all of this was choking the life out of me. I just kept on faking it, all the time drawing more of what I didn't want into my life.

God wanted me to see the effects that this twisted process of "stinking thinking" produced in my life. He wanted to free me. This couldn't be at the expense of anyone else.

Forgiveness was the key. It unlocked the gate to my freedom. Continuing to forgive in light of one atrocity after another that takes place in our messed-up society was the spiritual path that I took to walk through the gates to total freedom.

After taking this journey with the Lord, looking at my reflection in that spiritual mirror, I fell on my knees and asked for forgiveness

of God for all the backed-up garbage that I had allowed to settle in
my soul.

This rude awakening by God through my Jonah moment caused
so many questions for me. Why was God so patient with Jonah? I
believe He felt Jonah's pain. Just like my painful past, I believe God
understood the sensitive nature of Jonah's feelings because of his experiences that cut off his breath and mutilated his heart when he even
thought about the people of Nineveh.

God also knew that the people of Nineveh were the children of
Noah. God made a covenant with Noah just like He did with Abraham. He wouldn't keep a promise for one and not the other. Every
promise with God is guaranteed and sealed for fulfillment.

In my case, God has a covenant with white people, too. He didn't
just come to set black people free from our oppression. We're all
oppressed. Sin deprives us of the free life promised by Jesus Christ.

Baptism saves us for eternity, but forgiveness unlocks salvation in
the mind today. The longer we wait to demonstrate the power of this,
the longer we live in torment by forces that don't care anything about us.

How many times did God have to forgive the children of Israel?
It's too many to count. They made idols and then worshipped them.
That was sin number one. The first commandment of the Ten Commandments is, "You shall have no other gods before Me." But the laun-
dry list of sin baggage carried by the chosen people is long and sordid.

That's why Jesus had to come. He had to die. He knew that if
He exercised His authority to come off the cross, we'd never have a
chance. Repentance without His blood sacrifice would mean nothing.

Billy Graham preached repentance, just like Jonah, but his message was to unbelievers. Through his efforts, many came to know
Jesus. His ninety-nine years were impactful for that time.

This time, God and our Savior require repentance to come first from His Church, especially from those who lead who have run amok with His true values. He's putting us in check, and He needs to.

The Church is no place for hate.

The Church is no place for hidden agendas.

The Church is no place for hurting the flock.

The Church is no place for abuse.

This next move of God is not going to look like the past. That time is gone. God wants to move in another way now. Ecclesiastes 7:10 from the NIV says this: "Do not say, 'Why were the old days better than these?' For it is not wise to ask such questions."

Why do we keep looking back when God moves ahead, not backward? God is only in the past because of our memories of the old days. Our eyes must be firmly set on Jesus and what He wants to do *next*.

Repeatedly, His message is the same. God says, "Behold, I will do a new thing; now it shall spring forth; shall ye not know it? I will even make a way in the wilderness, and rivers in the desert" (Isaiah 43:19 KJV).

He says, "Shall ye not know it?" That speaks to our resistance in His process. But He doesn't leave us there. He precedes this statement with "It shall spring forth" because He has to do it suddenly before we object to it.

"This is the way it's always been done. Why do we have to change?" That's our answer to God—not people.

We've all been praying for God to move—to do something—but when He answers, we resist. Why is that?

In our desperation, we lose sight of what's really important. In our attempt at this life, we believe it's all about us. Everywhere that we look, the message is clear: "You can have it your way."

That's Burger King's slogan, not God's. He never told us that we can have it our way. He said, "Follow me." That's a clear directive.

How do we fumble that message? It's our interpretation of it, right? It's because of free will that we assume that when it comes to living for God, it works that way also.

We believe that we chose Him, and because we chose Him, we can pick and choose *how* we follow Him. We can haphazardly worship Him. We neglectfully serve Him, because we definitely hate our neighbor, and I mean that in the broadest sense of the word *neighbor*. That includes family.

Your daughter, who grew up in your home loving God, confesses that she's homosexual. You hate her because of it. Her choice of that lifestyle, which you know to be wrong, is no greater a sin than you hating her. But your hate is enraged against her—so much so that you refuse to be in her company ever again.

Would Jesus do that? Absolutely not. I believe that if Jesus were to walk the earth today, he would still rub the religious the wrong way. They would try to kill Him all over again.

In my imagination, religious leaders of today would come to Jesus with all their questions regarding the sins that we see today, like abortion, homosexuality, divorce, etc., and Jesus would silently bend down, writing in the sand, just as He did before. After their rants, Jesus wouldn't even look up as He commented, "You that are without sin, cast the first stone."

Then after the accusers were gone—those that were guilty of these sins—Jesus would turn to the outcasts, saying, "Where are your accusers? If there are none, I don't judge you either. Go and *sin no more*."

We forget that all sin separates us from God. That's why we need the blood of an innocent Lamb—Jesus.

Jesus, the maker of the law, came to nail the law to the cross so that sin can no longer hold us captive. He demonstrates His autonomy and control of all situations—whether seen or unseen by us, it doesn't matter. What matters is that we do not lose sight of what's important.

The Church government has become, in many instances, fruitless. It resembles Jude 12 (NIV): "These people are blemishes at your love feasts, eating with you without the slightest qualm—shepherds who feed only themselves. They are clouds without rain, blown along by the wind; autumn trees, without fruit and uprooted—twice dead."

The world needs evidence that God exists. That means the Church must wake up, come alive, and drive the car from the crime scene. It's a mess, but it's our mess to clean up.

Jesus sacrificed His life for what? This? Absolutely not. He gave His life so that we can be free—not enslaved again to those old patterns of living as judge and jury. He wants us to let love be the judge. Would *love* say that? Would *love* lock them out? Would *love* say I don't want to ever see you again? I think not.

The state of the world is our fault. We're walking around with our eyes closed to every dark situation going on around us. We talk about how bad things have gotten, but we do nothing to change course. We act as if nothing has happened.

Every time God pivots us back in His direction or changes the course for us, we go along for the ride for a while, then we revert to our old ways of doing things.

We see governments rise and fall based on who's in control. We even have the religious elite that will claim a candidate to be righteous who has nothing right about him, but they want to kill a doctor who performs abortions. What's the justification for this madness?

They'd rather have a young pregnant girl who knows she can't go home to tell her parents she's pregnant go to a woman's house to have an abortion and end up dying from infections. That's two deaths. Can you feel the sense of insanity that our stinking thinking has brought us to?

It's time for a change. A changing of the guard. An adjustment in who's in control.

One of the most prevalent concerns of God is the governmental order of His Church. In Jeremiah 3:15, God said, "Then I will give you shepherds after My own heart, who will feed you knowledge and understanding."

What is God's nature? God is love. He created its meaning, and there's no real love without Him. He's just, compassionate, forgiving, slow to anger, long-suffering, and faithful. Are those qualities of a good leader? Sure they are. That's what the Lord meant when He said shepherds after His own heart. The shepherds will have these same attributes.

God has already picked them out as He begins this new wind of change. Don't be shocked by the testimonies of strippers falling under the power of the Spirit right in the club where they used to dance. Or the attestation of those who received the Holy Spirit right in their homes. There was no worship service that they attended or good sermon. It was just them and the Spirit of God in their living room, then everything changed.

Don't be surprised when you hear the stories of thieves, murderers, and gangsters giving up their lifestyles because the Holy Spirit hit their lives with such power that it resembles Saul's experience on the road to Damascus.

Just as God birthed the nation Israel from twelve tribes and Jesus birthed His kingdom on earth with twelve apostles, Jesus is birthing something new and creative now. So be careful where you land while Jesus shifts and sifts us like wheat. You don't want to get caught in God's wrath as this wind blows, as it did in the case of Ananias and Sapphira. It's the wind that comes to cleanse and refine everything in its way. Just as there were consequences for Jonah's disobedience, there are repercussions for us. Just like Jonah, we can't run away from what God has called us to do.

It's time to end the political wrangling among houses of faith. Stop influencing the congregants to follow anyone other than Jesus—and He's not running for any office. He gave His life to save us. We are subjects of His kingdom, and there is only one king. Let's reorder our lives through our repentance and confession of sins so we can obtain mercy.

There's been a cycle of idol worship, where men and women of the cloth allow their followers to worship them instead of Jesus, who is our Savior. It's time to repent of exalting yourselves above God. Don't wait for the wrath of God to destroy you and everything in your path. It's not worth the little that you gain from it. Eternity is a long time to spend in hell, and don't assume that because you call on the name of Jesus you are an automatic shoo-in to heaven. The Word of God says:

> Many will say to Me on that day, "Lord, Lord, did we not prophesy in Your name, and in Your name cast out demons, and in Your name perform many miracles?" And then I will declare to them, "I never knew you; leave Me, you who practice lawlessness." (Matthew 7:22–23)

Don't waste this moment. Use it to give God the glory He deserves by being obedient in this hour.

Jesus started with twelve men leading His Church in its infancy to create the necessary order to authentically reach the world. Don't despise small beginnings. For more than two thousand years, the Church has remained as relevant as it was on the day of Pentecost. In fact, the Gospel has spread around the world and will continue until the day Jesus returns with power because the kingdom of God is like yeast that permeates the entire lump of dough.

The time is well spent, and we need to give an account of the state of the universal community of believers that we call the Church. Jesus is concerned about the order of His Church and the lack of care for those who are actually sheep. Let's come to the table with more than just conversation. We have the Holy Spirit as our strategist. We must use His strategies to start again.

We must choose truth over tradition, so don't let religion trip us up. The truth is that Jesus is the only Head of the Church. The order of it must be reorganized as you would reorganize a company that is failing to meet its financial goals. Those who need to step down will do so or be forced out so that God's newly chosen can step into positions of leadership as Jesus steers us in the direction He designed. There's still autonomy among the local churches, but that is insignificant when we serve the King as His subjects. It's His order that brought it all into existence, and it's by that same order that He will sustain it.

Just as Jesus plucked twelve men out from the world to follow Him, He comes again looking for a few good men and women who will sacrifice their lives to take up His life—those who will lead from their knees. With a few people, Jesus changed the world order, and it's time for a new world order again, but not as the world supposes.

Just as He turned over the money changers' tables because they were selling the sacrificial animals to those who failed to plan for their annual atonement sacrifice, Jesus comes with the same fury in His eyes as He asks the question, "Why do you come in My name when you're only interested in your own agendas?"

Let us rend our hearts with fasting and praying as we repent and return to our first love. We need to go back to the heart of worship. The Gospel has to be the central message, and it's heard the loudest when we live it. It is in our brokenness that there is hope.

We have prayed for a move of God. What if this is it? Like Jonah, let the change begin with us. "For it is time for judgment to begin with God's household; and if it begins with us, what will the outcome be for those who do not obey the Gospel of God?" (1 Peter 4:17 NIV).

If you lead a congregation, it's not too late for you. Repent today. Don't wait. Do it now. God knows your heart and is ready to use you for this next move He's making. The ball is in your court. What are you going to do with it?

4

INSIDE JOB

*I'll give you a new heart, put a new spirit in you. I'll
remove the stone heart from your body and replace
it with a heart that's God-willed, not self-willed. I'll
put My Spirit in you and make it possible for you
to do what I tell you and live by My commands.*

EZEKIEL 36:26–27 MSG

When I was a teenager, it was popular to increase your age. If you were fourteen, you would say that you were fourteen and a half, or "I'm about to be fifteen," and so on and so forth. It's an embellishment of the truth.

Somehow, this statement would make you feel older and more mature because your real age was never good enough. You were always reaching for the next rung on the ladder of life. The goal was to be grown, so there was a never-ending attempt to escape your reality.

In high school, I wanted desperately to go for "bad" although I was always considered a good girl. I wanted to lead a double life—or so it went down in my own mind.

I wanted to be one of the girls that hung out in the bathroom smoking and telling lies because telling lies was my favorite pastime.

I wanted to make my own life appear dark and sordid rather than the real story of my life as one raised in a strict Christian family where you were indoctrinated with all of the rules for living.

All of the *do not's* of life. The rules such as girls *do not* wear pants—Christian girls only wear dresses; they *do not* smoke; they *do not* drink; they *do not* curse; and they certainly *do not* lie.

I thought I was pretty good at lying until I hung out in the bathroom and happened upon girls who were better at it than I was—or so I thought they were lying. Many of them were lying, but there were some for whom I found out later in life the stories they told were real.

Some of them went home to what my mother used to call "a living hell." The bathroom experiences that we shared were their escape from reality, too. Home *was* hell for them.

So, we would bask in our momentary chances at a new reality, but eventually, teachers or the principal would run us out because we stayed in the bathroom longer than the "law" allowed us to. Then it was back to reality—back to class. Back then, truant officers were *really* intrusive and went to your house when you missed classes. My parents weren't going for that! You know. I had to keep my double life going—bad girl (on the surface) at school and a saint at home.

Do you know people like that? They're one way in public, but behind closed doors, they're someone else. They're so busy working to impress others. Which version of themselves is the *real* one?

Real is rare. Sometimes the real story isn't so interesting. It won't make movies. It doesn't sell books. Being honest with yourself is where you start the process of being authentic.

Transparency makes room for change. It becomes a confession, and in transparency, the heart decides to pivot.

What about transparency with God? You can fake it with people, but not with God. He already knows who you are. It doesn't matter if you are a bishop or a layperson—you are known fully by God.

When Jesus came on the scene of our world, He came turning everything upside down and inside out—including how we see things. Religion said that only certain people were qualified, and much of the qualification came from what you saw on the outside. You know, you had to dress a certain way, talk a certain way, and follow the rules and certain traditions.

Jesus came with a different message. He wanted to know people from the inside out—not the other way around. He didn't care what the outward appearance was. In fact, sometimes He was drawn to the ones outcast from society.

In Luke 18:10–14, Jesus tells the story about a Pharisee and a tax collector. In today's view, it would be a priest or bishop and a politician. You may have heard or read this parable from the Bible. It goes like this:

> Two men went up into the temple to pray, one a Phari-
> see and the other a tax collector. The Pharisee stood and
> began praying this in regard to himself: "God, I thank
> You that I am not like other people: swindlers, crooked,
> adulterers, or even like this tax collector. I fast twice a
> week; I pay tithes of all that I get." But the tax collector,
> standing some distance away, was even unwilling to raise
> his eyes toward heaven, but was beating his chest, saying,
> "God, be merciful to me, the sinner!" I tell you, this man
> went to his house justified rather than the other one; for
> everyone who exalts himself will be humbled, but the one
> who humbles himself will be exalted.

It's a new message. The "saint" is the sinner who doesn't know he's a sinner. He thinks too highly of himself. In puffing himself up, he becomes deflated by God, who sees what's not seen. In essence, God says the way to the top is by going down. It's through humility that God elevates us.

When we work to elevate ourselves, it is unbecoming. It's ugly and unappealing. No one likes to be around those who brag and boast about their own accomplishments.

How does this relate to a faith that is bulletproof? I believe it's twofold. On the one hand, there is grace for both the puffed-up saint and the humble sinner, but it's through the lens of grace that the puffed-up saint must humble himself—seeing fully his sinful state before grace is realized for him.

The other part is that the Pharisee must see himself as equal to the tax collector—not above or better than. He must make a striking parallel between them in such a way that he, too, beats his chest, confesses, "God, forgive me, THE sinner," then embraces the tax collector who wants to be forgiven. "The" is in all caps because we who are self-righteous teachers of God's law must recognize that we are chief of sinners. It is through this acknowledgment that we begin to understand how great a grace we have received.

For example, whether we admit it or not, we're all judgmental to some degree or another. That being said, who we are is not going to keep us from God's love. Nothing separates us from it.

What are the takeaways from this chapter? First, we need to clean our spiritual house from the inside out. This requires transparent and honest introspection. It's taking inventory of our lives and allowing the Holy Spirit to lead the clean-out process.

Secondly, stop judging other people. You don't have a right to sentence someone else when you don't understand what circumstances brought them to where they are today. Ask the Holy Spirit to lead you on how to change your heart in this area and how to transform it into something positive.

"For we wrestle not against flesh and blood..." I know you're quoting that Scripture with me before I can finish the statement. "...but against principalities, against powers, against the rulers of the darkness of this world, against spiritual wickedness in high places" (Ephesians 6:12 KJV).

Sometimes, the greatest enemy you fight is within you. You won't get out of the way of your own progress. You self-sabotage the work that can change everything. Those are mind battles, but don't engage in them. Use the Word of God to fight back by bringing your thoughts in line with what God says about you.

This is where a relationship with the Holy Spirit is critical. Jesus said, "Learn of Me." That's about relationships. In any relationship, you've got to spend time together, learning the likes and dislikes of the other person to know them.

A couple that's been married fifty years knows each other well enough that they can probably finish each other's sentences. This is probably not so with a young couple that just got married. Although they may have been together for some time, it's usually when you begin to actually live and share your life together that you know how a person will act under certain circumstances.

People can lie about who they are when the relationship is purely on the surface. They can appear to care deeply for you, but in actuality, they only tolerate you for selfish reasons.

Going deeper in your relationship with the Holy Spirit is what I'm talking about. You don't have to be all in when you start, but you've got to be determined that this is what you want.

If you're like me, I wasn't all in until I was all in. I didn't even know what I was choosing. I just knew something was pulling at me. It was tugging at my heart.

The more I knew, the more I wanted to know. Every bit of information that came my way drew me to want to discover more. I simply didn't realize what was just ahead for me.

Wanting more drew me to what appeared to be defeat. It took me into a wilderness experience. After September 11, 2001, my world was rocked, just as our nation was, because my husband became possessed by a demon.

We were scheduled to close our new house, but because of the attacks in New York and Washington, DC, on that fateful day, the closing was rescheduled for two weeks later. This delayed both the sale of our home that we were living in and the purchase of the new one.

The more I knew, the more I wanted to know.
Every bit of information that came my way
drew me to want to discover more.

Shortly after moving in, things began to change between my husband and me. We just didn't get along all of a sudden. He started hanging out with a new group of friends that I didn't know, and I noticed a gradual change in him.

Looking back, I can see that this is when our relationship shifted. I was growing closer to God, but he wasn't. We attended church services together regularly as a family, but we were growing apart spiritually.

The changes were ever so slight. We argued over insignificant things. He had his way of how he wanted things to be, and I had my way of how I wanted them to be. We just couldn't see eye to eye or find a compromise because we were both insistent on standing our ground.

We both were determined to have things done our way. I put pressure on him to be someone he was not, and in response, there would be a blowup, and then he would leave. Sometimes I felt that he picked fights with me just so he had an excuse to escape the prison that he felt our home had become. I say prison because I sensed his uneasiness around me as I also changed.

He felt trapped. As he was transforming, so was I. He didn't want God the way I did. There was nothing wrong with either of our positions, but our differences became an area of weakness. They became fertile ground for Satan to gain a foothold in our home.

I felt I had nowhere to turn for help. I wanted things to get better, but I felt hopeless and alone. I asked the prayer group that I participated with at my church what I should do, but they told me that demons couldn't possess Christians. All I knew was that when I looked at him, I saw a demon.

Then one day, a woman who had an appointment with me came into my office to do a mortgage loan application, and when she sat down, we began talking about her situation. The strange thing was that she wanted to refinance her current mortgage, but she hadn't brought in any of her mortgage documents. We only discussed the details of whom the mortgage was with, the loan amount, and other pertinent details.

Almost immediately, she began to share a word of knowledge with me. She mentioned that my brother had just died and that my mother was taking it very hard.

A tear rolled down my face. My mother wasn't the only one taking my brother's death rather hard. So was I. All of a sudden, it was as if no one else in the building existed but us. I lost sight of the fact that we were sitting in a glassed-in conference room on the first floor of the bank—not in my private office.

Then she mentioned my husband and our marital problems, and my sobs turned into a torrential downpour of tears. She prophesied about the things that were going to take place between us, our family, and our church.

At that point, I knew I had to move this meeting to another day. I became painfully aware of the eyes watching through the glass of the conference room. Not just other employees of the bank but customers were watching as I tried to gain my composure.

How did she know these things? This was the first time that I had met her, but she knew all about me. I needed to know more.

This chance meeting marked the start of my quest for discovery. As I look back, this was the beginning of my spiritual "boot camp"—the training ground where God planted people that understood spiritual warfare, including this woman that I now believe was an angel, in my path.

From this time, I learned how to effectively pray. I learned the art of spiritual warfare through the battles in my own home. I built my arsenal through fasting and praying—pushing until I saw a change in people and circumstances, including seeing demons leave my husband's body at the end of a nine-month period when the enemy made advances against me, but God taught me how to overcome through my prayers.

For approximately twelve years, people came in and out of our lives, teaching me the skills that impacted my development as an intercessor.

The last wrung of that training was under the tutelage of two bishops who came into our lives at the same time, first as customers and then as spiritual fathers. They heard from God and took charge to teach us everything that we needed to know about spiritual warfare. We received the Holy Spirit with evidence of speaking in tongues.

This was also the time when the enemy fought us the most to keep us from getting fully equipped in our development so that we wouldn't become what God originally intended for us to be. What I didn't know at the time was it was always a part of God's plan for it to work out just as it did.

The end of my boot-camp season came when a disagreement arose with one bishop because of a dispute over ministry matters, and the other bishop died. This caused an impasse where I went through one loss after another.

It began what looked like a downward spiral in my life. We had to move in with my mother after short selling our house. Our son, who was in the Air Force, became a wounded soldier after returning from the Middle East.

The next year, my mother was diagnosed with pancreatic cancer, and within four months she passed away. On the day that she passed away, the Holy Spirit stepped in to finish my spiritual boot camp.

It all began with a vision. It rocked me to my core because it hit my home and everything that I hold dear. It forever changed the course of my life and my understanding of who God is.

Right before seeing the vision, God told me that my husband was going to have an affair with a female coworker and that he would eventually leave me. He gave me her name, her husband's name, and her two minor children's names and ages. He also gave me the address where she and her family lived together and the address where she was going to move alone to.

Then the vision was of a man, for whom the Holy Spirit only gave a last name, and this woman riding in a car together. As they were driving past their office building, I saw my husband come out of the building and recognize that these two were together, and he then fell to the ground.

Holy Spirit made it clear that our marriage was over as we knew it, but He wanted me still to long for the relationship, waiting for God to complete His promise to me.

Then the Holy Spirit unveiled His intentions for restoration. He had spoken of restoring me several times over this same twelve-year period, but this time, He was more intentional with His choice of words.

God prepackaged this "deal" of a promise that He was restoring our marriage just as He's coming to restore His marriage with His Bride. He painstakingly caused me to wait two years before He would allow me to divorce my husband.

It was two years of watching the constant betrayal, but God knew that I would obey Him. He showed me the importance of sticking with it by paralleling my messed-up marriage with His. He seeks a human experience of His love that cuts to the core so that every one of us sees His pain and agony. This is not just so that we will pity Him but so that we will have a change of heart and lifestyle.

He knew all too well the level of pain that I was going through because He goes through more betrayal than I will ever dream of enduring. He just wanted to prepare me so that I would find hope in what He was offering me.

It was as if the wind had been knocked out of me. Nothing I'd ever been through could've prepared me for this. I was mourning both the dead and the living at the same time. It was a pain worse than death.

At the same time, God was doing an internal work in me. He caused me to lose approximately one hundred pounds within six months, and I have kept it off. He took the taste for bread, sugar, and sugary foods out of my taste buds along with incorporating a daily exercise routine that included a minimum of ten thousand steps a day.

He would get me up early—usually around three or four a.m. every morning—and have me go to the bathroom mirror, look deep into my own eyes, and tell myself how much I love Lauraine. He did this until I actually meant it.

Most times, I didn't want to do it. But He patiently got me up every day until one day, I said it and actually meant it. That day, I remember seeing a difference in my eyes as I said, "I love you, Lauraine...I really do."

Keeping a journal every day helped me to keep hope alive because God gave me private nuggets of Himself where He breathed new life into me—every day. I had something to hold on to as I struggled to get grounded again.

You know, hindsight is always 20/20, and now I can see that for one solid year, I wallowed in the pain of my position. I took on the role of a victim because of these attacks that came against me from every direction.

It took almost four years for me to fully get over what happened— my mother's death, my son's mental issues, my husband's betrayal, loss of businesses—all of it. Once I got over the heartache of it all, I realized—this is the meaning of the dream I shared at the beginning of the book:

Being in the car, I was spared direct gunshot wounds because I was powerless. The car was my safety net. I was upset for having to wait, but waiting didn't mean that I was to do nothing. It gave me a safe haven until the necessary work was completed. The internal work that I did with the help of the Holy Spirit sharpened me so that I became unshakeable through any situation.

That's the part that all of us as followers of Jesus need to take away from this dream. The Holy Spirit will direct us to do the internal work that we need to do so that we become the Church—the Bride that our Groom will be proud of when He returns. There will be no more roller-coaster rides. He's planting us on a firm foundation. Unshakeable. Unmovable. Abounding.

5

TARGET

*"Can a mother forget the infant at her breast, walk away
from the baby she bore? But even if mothers forget, I'd
never forget you—never. Look, I've written your names
on the backs of My hands. The walls you're rebuilding
are never out of My sight. Your builders are faster than
your wreckers. The demolition crews are gone for good.
Look up, look around, look well! See them all gathering,
coming to you? As sure as I am the living God"—GOD's
Decree—"you're going to put them on like so much
jewelry, you're going to use them to dress up like a bride."*

ISAIAH 49:15–18 MSG

S uddenly, I woke up to the sound of gunshots and the smell of
gunpowder. I couldn't recall having a dream, but I instantly
knew that there was a planned attack and children were in
danger. Startled by this awareness, I was eerily aware that my children were in jeopardy. It was Friday morning, September 29, 2006,
at about six o'clock a.m.

I immediately fell to the floor, praying and weeping. Sobbing
while crawling across my bedroom floor, I made a desperate cry for
my children's safety.

My oldest son was out of school, but I had a twelve-year-old daughter and a nine-year-old son. They both attended Mountain Park Elementary School, where just four years prior (February 2002) a guy had entered the school and randomly chosen to strike a fourth-grade girl in the head with a hammer. I was terrified of what could happen next and determined to painstakingly do whatever I had to do to protect what was mine.

I couldn't breathe. I immediately went into panic mode. I was desperate for God to hear my cry for help. I prayed like never before because even after waking up, I could still smell the gunpowder.

The memories of the Columbine massacre were still fresh as well, strikingly prevalent not just in my mind but also in the hearts and minds of all Americans. I cried for months thinking about those unsuspecting students and teachers who must've been gripped with fear of dying. My heart broke for the survivors and parents who lost their children, as well as for the entire community.

A piece of the fabric that makes up America was torn apart after this senseless carnage, and I'm not just speaking of the victims. Those two young men that did the shooting died senselessly as well. This was a watershed moment in our history, as we were waiting for responsible leadership to move us into a better reality, but that leadership never showed up.

During the three days after smelling gunpowder, I told everyone I knew to pray for our children and for the safety of children at all schools, specifically in Gwinnett County Schools, where my children attended. This fight I was in had become very personal.

I am a prayer warrior. I have been as long as I can remember. As such, when I pray, I don't stop until I feel a release in my spirit. During the three days after this experience, I still didn't feel the release as

I would normally. Each of the three nights afterward, I tossed and turned during the night, not able to rest well.

I was wrestling with something greater than myself, but I was trying to fight through this in my own strength—as you would fight most other fights. You fight with your fists. It was as if I had entered the ring of a wrestling match. I put my imaginary boxing gloves on, and I was swinging with everything within me.

They can't have my children. That was the intensity with which I fought this. I was just looking for those who would be willing to get in the ring with me. I knew this was a fight I didn't need to fight alone. What I didn't understand at the time was that I didn't need just anyone getting in the ring with me, but I needed to align with those who knew how to fight.

There were some people whom I asked to pray with me who thought I was hysterical for no good reason. They thought that I was letting my imagination get the best of me. After all, there had been so much hysteria after Columbine. Some of them felt that I was a little crazy. Some even thought that I probably ate too late before going to bed.

The only thing was that there had been times when I'd had troubling dreams and had been moved with the need to pray, but for whatever reason—distractions, disbelief, or ambivalence—I hadn't prayed, and later, things happened. I didn't want this to be one of those times, especially since I felt strongly that children were involved.

Then, on the following Monday afternoon, October 2, 2006, we heard the news reports that a shooting had occurred at the West Nickel Mines School, a one-room schoolhouse in an Amish community in Pennsylvania. Once I heard about it, I understood why I'd smelled the gunpowder.

Sometimes, you have to lose to learn. I tossed that dream around in my head for weeks, pondering every detail so that I would recognize the signs in the future. You must break apart the signs to get to the essence of the message.

The signs: gunpowder isn't used much today. If you hone in on that one piece of information, it was a clue pointing toward the Amish. That's called spiritual mapping.

It requires critical thinking, just as criminal investigators exercise when investigating a crime scene. Every piece of evidence either leads to more questions or to an answer.

So it is in spiritual warfare. The Holy Spirit gives us pieces at a time because that's all we can handle, and in hunting for answers we begin to learn the nature of God. "For we know in part and prophesy in part" (1 Corinthians 13:9).

Heaven sees what earth misses. We are so distracted that many times we can't see what's right in front of us. The Holy Spirit opens our understanding to what heaven sees so that, although distracted, we still see.

It's a process. The ability to hear and see things before they happen comes from having a relationship with the Holy Spirit. Some of us were given this gift at birth. We could always see things in advance. For others, it's our thirst for God that causes Him to send answers.

For me, I was given the gift at birth, but it was suppressed by religion. In spite of their efforts, I was thirsty. Through time and trials, wrestling and wrangling, my life intersected with the knowledge of who the Holy Spirit is, and I wanted to know more.

Mind you, this desire was real, and it originated from heaven. I couldn't boast about being thirsty because God made me thirsty. I just followed.

I joined a prayer ministry and began learning how to pray effectively. In the beginning, we were somewhat intimidated by those who appeared to be better at it than we were. Again, it was about appearances—not what was real.

We went down rabbit holes that produced little fruit. Prayer ministers who were well-spoken and overzealous for titles and to be out front found our gullible positions easy prey. That's where religion suppressed the gifts that I was given. Discerning whom to associate with is very important.

Then life circumstances pushed me over the edge. I needed prayer strategies for the spiritual warfare that I was entrenched in. What they were offering couldn't match what I was dealing with on my own.

Demons moved into my house. They took over my husband. The prayer ministers that I was subject to had no experience with such. They told me demons cannot possess Christians. They were wrong, and I had evidence of it. I just didn't know who I was then. I cowered to their leadership because I didn't know any better.

But God did. He sent people and angels to teach me the art of spiritual warfare. It's an art because each of us brings sets of circumstances different from everyone else that make us passionate about prayer.

During this time, a woman who came to work for me at the bank became one of those teachers. At the church that I grew up in, they mainly taught from the New Testament, so I never really read much of the Old Testament. I began visiting this lady's Bible studies, and they opened me to study about things I had never heard of.

Fasting was a new concept for me. Reading about Daniel's fast moved me, and it was because I was at a pivotal moment in my life that this story meant something to me.

Daniel was a Jewish young man who was taken into captivity by King Nebuchadnezzar. His story is found in the self-titled book of the Bible.

Why did he practice fasting? It was a Jewish sacrament and was a tradition expected of any good Jew.

You may recall the stories in which Daniel interpreted dreams, saw visions, and was thrown into the lion's den. All of these things brought him promotions and accolades. But it was his thirst for God that was most impactful.

Daniel chose to live by God's standard set for His people. He ate a limited diet although the choicest of foods were reserved for him and the three Hebrew boys.

In Daniel 9, we observe the first mention of a fast. Daniel read the prophecies of Jeremiah regarding the exile of Jerusalem and decided to inquire of God. He confessed his sins and the sins of his people that had caused their exile.

For twenty-one days, according to Daniel 10, Daniel fasted. He ate no meat, drank no wine, and no ointment was used on his body. By the twenty-fourth day, Daniel had a disturbing vision that caused a deep sleep to come over him. Then an angel brought the answer he was seeking. It took three weeks for the angel to show up, but he was on his way to Daniel from the moment Daniel prayed to God.

Why is that important? Because God always answers the prayers of the righteous, but there are forces that work to delay delivery of those answers to us. They may be delayed but not denied.

This woman and I began praying over the phone at six a.m. every morning. She didn't know what I was going through, but because I was thirsty, I showed up for more and more every day.

One morning, I spilled the beans about my warfare with my husband, and she immediately said that it was time for us to fast. Fast?

Yep. We went for forty days with no food—only water—and we prayed together at six a.m. every morning.

One of the keys for me was that she told me to write down my prayers and pray them every hour. This was also the first time I heard about having the Holy Spirit. She asked me whether or not I had the Holy Spirit, and I told her that I had no knowledge of that. She said that she had Him and she would pray in the Spirit, and I would pray the prayers that I wrote down.

That's exactly what we did, and the last week of our fast, I could barely walk. It felt as though I was about to deliver a baby. I walked wide legged and experienced extreme pressure in my thighs and lower back. I was birthing out something that I had never seen before, and I was living with anticipation for what was coming next.

The Sunday of the last week of the fast, a woman came into our worship. At the end of the sermon, my brother, our pastor, opened up for visitors who wanted to make comments, and this woman stood up. She said that she was on her way to another church, but the Spirit told her as she was about to pass ours to turn in at this church. She said while driving into the parking lot, the Spirit had told her to tell someone that their prayers are moving heaven and that the answer will come forth like having a baby.

I knew that message was for me because I had given birth to three children. I knew that pressure was the feeling of childbearing. Also, the forty-day fast ended the following Friday. Nothing just happens. This was a sign of what was and what was to come.

That week, my husband wouldn't come home. As my fasting and praying intensified, so did his behavior. By Friday, he was reeling from demonic attacks that flooded his mind with thoughts of suicide.

He called me that Friday night. I could tell from his voice that he wasn't stable. The first thing he said was, "I messed up." I told him to come home. I said that whatever it was, we could get through it. But he refused.

He didn't come home until Saturday in the wee hours of the morning. I didn't know exactly what he was wrestling with at the time, but I knew it was heavy because I couldn't sleep.

As he sat down on the chair in our bedroom, he slumped down, weeping. Again, he said, "I messed up." As I sat up in bed, he moved from the chair to the window seat. I was speechless. I just stared as I watched demons leave his body and float out of the window.

The fast was over. Now the demons had to leave. They had to let him go, and one of my prayers had been that I wanted to see them leave. I got my wish.

I was never the same after that day. I knew I needed more. I wanted the Holy Spirit. I wanted to understand how fasting and praying are more effective than prayer alone in some cases. I also knew that I would not learn the things that I was now thirsty for while sitting in the same church. They were not equipped to give me what I longed for.

I was speechless. I just stared as I watched demons leave his body and float out of the window.

Where could I go to quench *this* thirst? I went to the only source that had answers. I prayed and asked God for direction. He sent my husband and me to two churches where we worked as leaders and were equipped with the keys that unlock the kingdom of heaven. A part of that equipping was fasting and praying.

What about you? Have you ever fasted before? What was the outcome? If you haven't, why not?

When I started this journey, I had no living human example of the results you read about in the Bible. That's what I was thirsty for. I was looking for someone alive today with an eyewitness account that God had done for them what He did for those written in the pages of the Word.

My issue was that if God is alive, shouldn't we have current examples—not just historical ones—of His power to save us from the here and now? When I asked those questions, I didn't expect that I would become that example.

What is fasting? It is voluntarily abstaining from food and drink for a period of time. When fasting for spiritual reasons, it can also encompass avoiding electronics, television—whatever things attract your flesh the most, thereby slaying those things in the flesh that distract us from the things of God.

Fasting is more than just preparing your heart. It is a process of denying yourself. Your priorities shift. It's more of God and less of you.

Fasting causes God to shake up heaven and earth just because one person dared to believe. When fasting, it's important to approach it with childlike faith. You don't just hope for better to come. You know God will answer.

Fasting has immense implications that we need to understand. Fasting is not just about us getting what we want. It changes us as much as it moves God. Our prayers that come out of fasting are amplified for God because He sees our motivation.

Fasting is an extreme demonstration of our faith in God. It's out of desperation that we fast, when our other efforts produce little to no signs of an answer. Fasting pushes us to do what is unnatural. Going without food says I want change more than I want to fill my belly.

What's the "low-hanging fruit" for us regarding fasting? It's a faith-filled illustration of our need for God to move. Start fasting for one or two days then build up the number of days that you can go without food.

When you exit the fast, be sure to gradually reintroduce foods back into your diet. You don't want to shock your digestion by taking in too much too soon. Go slowly by adding the calories back a little more each day.

Prepare before beginning a fast. What's the purpose of your fast? How long will you fast for? Do you need a partner when you pray? If so, find someone willing to commit to fasting and prayer with you. Sit with the Holy Spirit and ask for direction on how to pray. Do as I did when beginning by writing down your prayers so that you effectively cover everything that the Spirit gives you.

Will you fast from food or will you fast from electronics use? Electronics use is so prevalent that it's a great option to start out with. Try going one day without social-media use and see how you do. During those times that you want to take a peek at Instagram, just know that is a time that you need to pray and seek the Holy Spirit's help.

You can do this. The world is waiting for you to be the beacon of light that it needs. Your prayers and fasting will move the mountains that need to be moved so that you are the change that the world is so desperate for.

6

BETWEEN ROCKS

Do not fear, for I have redeemed you;
I have called you by name; you are Mine!
When you pass through the waters, I will be with you;
And through the rivers, they will not overflow you.
When you walk through the fire, you will not
be scorched, nor will the flame burn you.

ISAIAH 43:1-2

I feel the squeeze as my chest tightens with fear. My heart is beating out of control. My heart rate has increased, and I'm sweating profusely. I feel the struggle to breathe as I'm panting heavily. As the lane barriers close in on us, I feel sweat roll down my back.

There's only one lane, and it has walls on both sides of it. They're doing major infrastructure and highway work that requires concrete walls to be installed on each side of the lane, separating drivers from the area where they're working. We're in between rocks.

There are no warning signs. We just run right smack dab into a construction site, with nothing preparing us for what we were approaching.

Why am I so afraid? It's the fear of an accident. My youngest son is driving, and I'm already apprehensive about his driving. That knowledge alone puts me between rocks. This, coupled with traveling a narrow, one-lane highway, stresses me out because there's no room for errors. I've heard horror stories of people running into walls on the highway, leading to their death.

Last, but not least, people drive so crazy these days. They don't care about anyone or anything except getting to where they're going as fast as humanly possible.

Also, what happens if a car breaks down on that one lane? Such a catastrophe would shut down traffic for hours. Having just one lane for all cars to travel brings traffic to a screeching halt when there are car breakdowns or accidents.

We all know that the public will benefit from the work that is being done on the highway. It will increase the number of lanes and make the ride smoother, with no uneven roads or potholes. It's just difficult moving through the process while they do the work.

Existing in a place that we call "between rocks" causes stress that's hard to navigate. The concrete walls on each side of the lane represent rocks, and the potential problems caused by only having one lane represent the hard place.

I'm all too familiar with hard places. I've had more than my fair share of difficulties. More than the law should allow. Navigating those times separates "the men from the boys." It separates the milk from the cream. The cream always rises to the top. It never settles.

I can remember my mother calling me one morning in the fall of 2000. She had a dream about me and my family that she didn't quite understand. She couldn't shake the way it made her feel—she became extremely anxious about this chilling dream. She gave a very descriptive account of the dream that was also puzzling for me at the time.

She dreamed that a huge boulder fell out of heaven and hit my home. She said that it was so devastating to her because the house was completely destroyed. The sight of it caused fear to grip her heart.

In all of the financial disasters that hit our lives, God was faithful to provide for every need. When a need arose, so did God's provision—every single time.

That feeling of devastation gave way to elation as she watched angels, one by one, fly from heaven to our home, and as they touched our house, light filled it, giving way to the rebuilding of the house piece by piece.

Obviously, this was a prophetic dream before we understood what that meant or we could fathom this happening to us, but it had significant meaning for my life and family.

If we had been taught that God really wants to speak to us today through dreams and visions, we would have asked probing questions about my mother's dream—not of the universe but of God. We would have realized that it was a guidepost—a sign of things to come. It was an angelic rescue plan orchestrated by God. As this dream became our reality, we lost sight of it and could've lost our way, but God…

The first boulder that hit our home was not long after the events of 9/11 rattled the very fabric of America. It rocked our *finances*. Our businesses one by one began to fail. Going from years as the owner of a company to begging for a job as a contractor was life-altering.

Although our income shriveled up and nearly died, we never lost anything. We were able to sell our home in a down economy and failed real estate market. In all of the financial disasters that hit our lives, God was faithful to provide for every need. When a need arose, so did God's provision—every single time.

The next boulder rocked our church. After worship one Sunday, a young lady that I love dearly stole my wedding ring. It wasn't just that she stole my ring. It was the meaning behind *that* ring. She knew our financial situation, and she also knew that my then-husband had sacrificed to buy me that ring for our anniversary.

He found it and put it on layaway for nine months before our anniversary to surprise me. She knew all of the details, yet she stole it anyway.

How did she know the intimate details of our lives? When she and her husband hit hard times and were forced out of their home, we allowed them to move into ours. Her decision to steal from those that came to help her hit me like a ton of bricks.

I was so ripped apart by this, but then my husband found the ring in a pawn shop that we used to frequent near our home while we were shopping for a replacement.

He recognized it immediately. He knew it was mine because of an insignia on the inside of the band.

She had pawned it at a pawn shop across town, probably fifty miles or more from our home, but it ended up six months later at the pawn shop right near us.

In order for us to get the ring back, I would have had to file a police report, and I really didn't want to do that. Instead, I called the young woman who stole it to inform her that we had found the ring in a pawn shop and that we knew that she'd pawned it.

In my heart, I just wanted to give her the opportunity to come clean about what she did. Of course, she continued to deny that she had any part in the disappearance of the ring. As I was speaking with her, I gained perspective and resolved to let it go.

I was just so hurt, and it reflected in how I responded. Because of that, I didn't pursue getting the ring back. I didn't file a police report because I still loved her, and I didn't want to go through having to prosecute someone that I loved.

The pawn shop had a record of where my husband had purchased the ring, and more than that, all of the employees knew us. They knew our story. They were so moved that the manager at the time offered that we could buy the ring back at a greatly reduced price, but I no longer wanted that ring. It carried with it a mark of tragedy that I didn't want to associate with my life any longer.

So, I let it go. The manager of the store, seeing our struggle and our dilemma, offered that if we bought another ring in their store, he would greatly discount it for us.

For weeks before my husband noticed the stolen ring in the store, I had been looking at a ring that was a thousand times better than the ring that was taken from me. All of our negotiations on that ring had been unsuccessful before. But because of our situation, the manager accepted our offer—which was lower than our original offer on the new ring—and allowed us to put it on layaway.

Then 2012 came, and the next boulders hit with a vengeance. This was a *bittersweet* year for us. Our son had a breakdown after coming back from serving in the Middle East while in the Air Force, we short sold our home, our daughter graduated from high school and then entered college, and we moved in with my mother for nine months before purchasing a new home.

All of that could've completely taken me out, but it didn't. God was still holding me and our lives together. You'll never know that God is all you need until He is all you have.

New Year's Eve that year, at the stroke of midnight, our bishop transitioned from this life to eternity, and spiritually we seemed bankrupt. At that time, it appeared that God had abandoned us. By all indications, things had completely fallen apart.

Of course, there were still some good things going on, but don't we tend to dwell on the negative when it seems like the floodgates of trouble have opened up over our lives? Our daughter was doing extremely well in college, and our youngest son was still in high school.

What we failed to notice was the gift of living with my mother. I can see it now, but I was crippled with defeat at the time, and that was nothing compared to what it did to my husband. His manhood and ability to take care of his family were jeopardized. But it was either live with her or rent a house until we could close on a new one.

At the time, the contract fell apart on the house we loved, so, we had to go back to the drawing board to find a new one, and that took a while—nine months to be exact.

In those nine months, something happened to me. I began noticing things about my mother that I'd never noticed before. She was retired, but she worked from sunup to sundown every day. If she wasn't cleaning, she was tutoring someone's child. If she wasn't tutoring, she was counseling someone's love life.

The first week that we moved in, she told me that it was the most restful night's sleep she had had since moving into that house. Prior to us moving in, she lived alone in a five-thousand-square-foot four-bedroom, three-and-a-half-bath home with a full basement. She lived in fear at night because she was there all alone.

She needed the feeling of protection and safety that our being there provided. God orchestrated our uncomfortable move to fulfill her needs. In return, we were blessed.

She was a powerhouse. She had so much joy and love for everyone that she came in contact with, and in watching her at work, I became a new woman. I went through a gradual transformation into a duplication of who she was.

I so desperately needed that change. I was suffocating from the years of painful and reckless life choices. The dumping ground which had become my life was unbearable. The stench alone would cause disease, but God got me to a hospital that was disguised as my mother's home. It was there that I was resuscitated, and my life was revived. At least, I was on life support and beginning to breathe on my own.

But the battle—the tug of war for my life—was only beginning. Just around the bend would be the ultimate test.

The most destructive of all boulders that hit our home happened in January 2014. My mother was diagnosed with pancreatic cancer, and by April, she had transitioned from this life to the next. By June, my husband had begun a love relationship with a co-worker and was on the brink of moving out of our home.

These things rattled the very foundation of my faith. How could a gracious and merciful God allow all of this to happen to someone who loved and trusted Him like I did? I had put all of my faith and trust in the idea that He would not abandon me when I needed Him the most. He would not allow such atrocities to happen to me.

Why would He tell me He was going to save me but allow so much tragedy to happen? It was in 2008 that I had a life-altering encounter with God like nothing I've ever had. As I was going about my day as

I always did, the Spirit of God blew on me and nearly knocked me off my feet. Yes, I said knocked me over.

As I was gathering myself immediately afterward, I went to the bathroom to splash water on my face. I looked in the mirror, and my face was flushed. As I touched my face, I heard the Spirit of God say to me, "I am restoring you, and I am beginning the restoration with your husband."

Yes, He showed me in advance that He would restore me, but He didn't tell me what that meant. He didn't tell me that my life would have to fall apart for Him to restore it. He didn't tell me that everything and everyone I loved and held dear would be ripped from me. He didn't warn me that everything around me was going to be shattered.

He only told me the end result, but the boulders still hit our finances, family, marriage, children, and then our faith. That's when God stepped in, and my one-on-one spiritual boot camp started.

The Spirit told me many things that day that I rehearsed and played back over and over again during my wilderness time. Those words kept me going.

A part of what He said was that the restoration of my marriage would mirror what He is doing for His Church—restoring it to its rightful place as His Bride.

What will that restoration look and feel like? I believe it will be just as painful and gut-wrenching as what I went through.

The Church is between a rock and a hard place. The Rock is Jesus. The hard place is religion.

It's religion that must be transformed. The power of the Rock has no appeal to the world because of religion and those who lead it.

When COVID-19 upended our lives in 2020, the Church was at an impasse. No one knew how to proceed. Church leaders were between a Rock and a hard place. The Rock, which is Jesus, always has concern for the sheep, but religion dictated that many congregations stay open.

Why? What did they have to prove? People were dying left and right, but their main concern was *tithes and offerings*. They believed that their congregants would only give because of their exceptional grandstanding. Therefore, many refused to close the doors of their buildings.

No one was asking them to shut down for good—just opt to stay connected over Zoom or some other platform instead of exposing the members to the threat of spreading the disease. Was that too much to ask for?

Instead, from their pulpits they belittled those churches that resorted to connecting with their congregants remotely. They claimed that those pastors had no faith in God. As if churches needed to compete, they purported that how they dealt with the pandemic was a test of faith.

It was more about having a shepherd's heart than a test of faith. Put under pressure, their true character was exposed to the light. A shepherd protects the sheep—he doesn't put extreme pressure to perform on them.

Corporations demonstrated more care for their employees than churches for their flock. They quickly assessed the needs of the company and made accommodations for employees to work remotely. Why was this so difficult for church leadership?

Church leaders tried to conceal their true identity: wolves disguised as shepherds. They claimed COVID-19 was a work of Satan, but it revealed who they were and their real intentions.

The true test of faith was believing that God would provide for the financial needs of the Church no matter what came their way. But the show must go on, right?

It was January 2022, and just as the New Year was ushered in, that the Spirit of God gave me a Word regarding September. He said, "Doomsday is upon you." I thought this was related to the promises that He had made about restoring me, but I wasn't sure of it.

Like putting together puzzle pieces, when the Lord reveals another piece, I try to figure out where the new piece goes in regard to the big picture. The only way to know for sure is to ask. When I asked the Holy Spirit for understanding, this was His response:

> It's a time of swift transition. Don't be moved by what you see and hear. The clock is ticking, and all things are aligned. You will begin to see evidence of what I promised. The dominoes are falling fast. Prepare for launching.
>
> My Church is clueless. It's grappling for straws instead of seeking Me with repentance and reverence for the things that are most important to Me—not religion. Again, I say, My people are destroyed for a lack of knowledge.
>
> Doomsday is upon you, and there's no more time for frivolous activity. With intention and focus, look for the sign, then My answer will be revealed to you.

God is putting religion on notice. Change or be destroyed from the inside out. There is only one Head, and His name is Jesus. He says, "Just as I said before, I can raise new children from these stones. You believe that you can do whatever you want to do in My name and that I will back you up. That's the reason I have given you over to your dastardly deeds. I allowed you to keep up your debauchery, but your day of reckoning has come," says the Spirit of God.

I challenge anyone in a leadership role at a church that carries the name of Jesus as its Savior to repent today. You know what that means. Confess your faults—not just to the Savior but also to your congregation—and turn from your way to the Way, Jesus. Your sins were public, and you must repent publicly. Fast and pray for Him to restore you because He will restore order to His Church—with or without you. Don't become a casualty of war.

7

VIEW FROM THE VALLEY

*Yea, though I walk through the valley of the shadow
of death, I will fear no evil; for You are with me.*

PSALM 23:4 NKJV

don't believe in God." That's what they both told me. This was
coming from my adult children that I raised to love God. We took
them to church every Sunday, read our Bible, prayed with and for
them. They attended Sunday School every week and went through
an extensive study of who God is. How could they not believe?

It takes courage to ask this question—Is God real? Everything
created started with asking a question. And what I know about this
human experience is that everything starts and ends with God. If a
question is asked, He has the answer to it.

Where did we go wrong? I was speechless. How should I respond?
After no words, I became angry at them. How do you go from believing in God to not believing? What causes your doubts?

Is God real? Does our doubt cancel out His truth? A good portion
of the population of the world asks this question, and it is a very important one to ask. God isn't afraid of our questions, but He's disappointed
in the answers that we're not able to give in response to the question.

Most times, this question comes after enduring catastrophes or painful events that shake us to the core. Family tragedies, fatal attacks on communities that are senseless, or cancer coming to take a loved one all cause us to question God's existence. I call those times valley experiences.

What is a valley?

> Valleys are depressed areas of land—scoured and washed
> out by the conspiring forces of gravity, water, and ice.
> Some hang; others are hollow.[4]

Isn't it interesting the choice of words used to describe the valley? Depressed areas...washed out...conspiring forces...some hang... hollow. These are also descriptive of what life looks like in the valley.

But which came first, the mountains or the valleys? I believe the mountains did, but before either was created, God separated the waters. That's how earthen matter formed as we know it.

Water is what causes the valleys to appear between mountains. As water moves, mountainous areas get washed out, and over time it causes disintegration of rock and earthen matter, which develops into areas where water can reside. As the waters subside, valleys appear.

Valleys exist all around the world. They are low-lying areas of land that are usually surrounded by hills or mountains. They come to be after a slow erosion of land occurs and become a place for farming due to their flat composition with soil that's ripe for cultivating.

At night, the valley can be scary. During young David's time, a shepherd watching over his flock in a valley at night was open to

4. "Valleys," *National Geographic*, nationalgeographic.com/science/article/valleys.

become the prey of beasts. It's tough to fight off beasts while in the valley because of the distorted view.

In Psalm 23:4 (KJV), David says: "Yea, though I walk through the valley of the shadow of death, I will fear no evil: for Thou art with me; Thy rod and Thy staff they comfort me." With imagery of this place from the perspective of sheep living in the valley, we are summoned to see the darkness. It calls us to feel the cold dampness of a night in the valley. It becomes the "valley of the shadow of death" due to the predators that stalk at night with the intention of killing the sheep.

Can you picture it? Creeping eyes peeking through the brush, longing for the night's dinner—and that intended dinner is you. Fear creeps in. It's the fear of the unknown. You need protection, and it comes from a good shepherd—not a lazy one. This kind of shepherd requires little to no sleep because he needs to protect the sheep from predators that creep by night and those that prey from the air during the day. His job is never done.

That's why the rod and staff were of comfort. They symbolize authority, power, and protection. The rod wielded against predators ensured the safety of the sheep. The staff was a tool to count the sheep and to guide them when they wandered off.

David understood that it takes a good shepherd to navigate the valleys without losing any sheep. It's a balancing act. He had to time everything just right. He had to know when to go through the valleys to ensure the safety of all sheep. It would be in the spring or fall of the year that the shepherd would herd the sheep on the trek through the valley in order to get to pastures for grazing in the winter and summer months.

Seasons change, and so does the scenery. The timing of my adult children's questions of God's validity is the "springtime" of their lives.

They moved from my house of rules to create their own homes, where they get to choose what rules to keep and which they will throw away. They get to reconcile all relationships—including the one with God. They're in a valley season of life.

It's in the valley that our core beliefs are rocked and reshaped. We come to the valley when the challenges of life shift our journey of seeking answers to probing questions. When none seem to appear, we banish the thoughts.

"Yea, though I walk through the valley of the shadow of death, I will fear no evil." I grew up learning to recite this Scripture from the twenty-third psalm, but the full measure of its meaning didn't impact me until the last few years.

How could David say this with such assurance? Where did he find the power to make such a bold statement that even though he walks through the valley of the shadow of death he could fathom having no fear?

As I experienced my own valley encounters, I was fearful. I became immobile—just couldn't seem to move ahead without help. That led me to ponder this familiar Scripture instead of just reciting it. I needed a better understanding so that I too could encounter God in that way.

I didn't question God, but those around me pushed my understanding to make me think about the notion that God causes circumstances that lead to valleys and shadows of death and dying. Could this be true?

Although I tossed this idea around in my head, I immediately scolded myself because I knew better, but I began to look for evidence of what I believed.

My daughter made a statement to me as we experienced some really tough times that made me push for answers. She said, "What good is religion if it can't be challenged? Your confidence in God has little meaning if it can't be questioned. You should be able to defend what you believe."

I shook as she said it. My heart resonated with her intention. Truer words have not been spoken. It came "out of the mouth of babes."

This is her reality. She's looking for answers, too. She's questioning whether God is as good as we say He is. We raised her to love Him, but now, as an adult, she's confronted with an existence that pushes back against this truth. She sees life now through the lens of hardships that have a way of rolling down hills and hitting you like a ton of bricks.

> She sees life now through the lens of
> hardships that have a way of rolling down
> hills and hitting you like a ton of bricks.

She's experienced unanswered prayers—or just not the answers she was expecting. Therefore, He can't be all that good. I believe that she's not the only one who sees God this way.

If she's looking, then I want to find the answers, because I need her to know what I believe with all of my heart. That is, that God is the Good Shepherd, and He only wants the best for us. That's a mother's love for her child, but I'm also acting as a shepherd for her— my sheep. I cannot leave her with these questions unanswered—or worse, answered with thoughts opposed to what I believe. "Ravenous wolves" want to change her view of God.

I believe God doesn't do the dirty work in our lives. He cleans it up. The filthy, ridiculous, and contemptible acts that occur in our lives are perpetrated by one force, and it's not God. Those dirty deeds have Satan's name written all over them.

In my search for answers to her questions, I found that a shepherd lives with a singular focus—the sheep and their well-being. His entire existence centers around preparing for their needs, such as food, water, and safety—even recreation.

What does all the talk about the valley mean to a shepherd? He can't allow taking the route through the valley, with all of its dangers, to cause harm to his sheep. They're his most precious and priceless possessions. He knows valleys are unavoidable, and it's not just his abilities that can keep them safe. He must trust in the power of God to keep both him and the sheep safe at all times, but especially through the valley.

You remember the saying that God will take what the enemy meant for evil and turn it for our good?[5] I conclude that's what God did in David's lifetime that launched his language in Psalm 23 to describe with such confidence God saving him from death while going through the valley. And my children will have the same testimony.

I imagine that it was probably while in the valley that David encountered the lion and the bear. I believe that God used the valley experiences of David, where he had to learn how to fight to protect the innocent lambs that his father charged him with (1 Samuel 17:20–58). Without the struggle to save the sheep from the ravages of hungry lions and bears, he wouldn't be prepared for the fight of his life.

The valley experience was the training ground for greatness. Ultimately, it was because of how David acted during his time in the valley that God confidently chose him for his position as a warrior and king.

---

5. Genesis 50:20.

That fight with Goliath was one of David's greatest valley out-comes, where he passed the test. That battle happened in the valley (1 Samuel 17:52). The experiences conquering valley periods in his life made him bold and unapologetic, causing him to rise out of the wreckage of woeful times. In fact, he was brazen as he prayed these faith-filled words to God in the form of a declaration about Goliath (1 Samuel 17:45–47 NKJV):

> Then David said to the Philistine, "You come to me with a sword, with a spear, and with a javelin. But I come to you in the name of the LORD of hosts, the God of the armies of Israel, whom you have defied. This day the LORD will deliver you into my hand, and I will strike you and take your head from you. And this day I will give the car-casses of the camp of the Philistines to the birds of the air and the wild beasts of the earth, that all the earth may know that there is a God in Israel. Then all this assem-bly shall know that the LORD does not save with sword and spear; for the battle is the LORD's, and He will give you into our hands."

Prayer was David's weapon on that battlefield. All of the other men of Israel were equipped with the same power, but they failed to use it because they didn't know how to apply it. They didn't see a need for God in these circumstances.

They probably saw God as a genie in a bottle because God always seemed to come in the nick of time. Before going into battle, they usu-ally consulted the prophet instead of going directly to God. Because of the prophet's relationship with God, the seer (as they were called), through his seeing gifts, told them whether God would be with them or not.

They didn't have a personal relationship with God. They didn't understand "men ought always to pray." That's where the power is. It's not in the muscles or weapons made with hands. That's what saved David. He used powerful prayers that were instinctive to him but not to others.

David wore no armor and carried no sword. He came to the battlefield with a slingshot, five stones, and his words of victory. It was through his valley experiences that he learned to travel light. He understood that the power was not in his might but in recognizing God's power to save through his faith in Him.

But then there's the cleft as you go through valleys, climbing up the side of the mountain, that helps you gain traction. In Exodus 33, Moses has a conversation with God as he is preparing to lead the children of Israel into the promised land. God tells him to leave Sinai and that He is sending His angel before them to fight the enemies that will come against them as they make their trip. He promises to take care of the enemies they haven't even encountered yet.

But as valley experiences often go, the people begin to complain and feel sorry for their circumstances. In this pitiful state, God calls them stiff-necked—noncompliant—always finding the negative. They don't trust that God can save them.

These are the same people that have just come out of Egypt, where God brought all the plagues against Egyptian citizenry but spared the Israelites from enduring the pain of the locust, the bloody water—even the death of the firstborn sons of the Egyptians. What Pharaoh means for their destruction—which should have been the pigeonhole for them to be captured and returned—God uses to show His power to save. He causes them to pass through the Red Sea, which at its deepest is thirty-six feet, on dry land and uses that same path to drown Pharaoh and his army. What is their salvation is the Egyptians' demise.

It's in the cleft of the mountain that God shelters Moses as He passes by after Moses asks to see His glory. Because of love, God covers him with His hand, knowing that if Moses sees His face, he will die. We don't understand that some things that we ask for can cause death, but God protects us because of our innocence. We don't know what we don't know.

God had to hide me in a cleft—a Rock, which is Jesus—so that He could pass by, showing me His glory. The cleft is where He made me become a servant. This wasn't about strictly serving. It meant that every title I held—vice president of a bank, entrepreneur, owner of a mortgage company, pastor, prophet—everything had to be stripped away until I complied with His plan for my life. I didn't understand at first, so He did it for me.

One by one, the titles fell away from me. Businesses closed—both mine and others. God made me uncomfortable in places of worship where He sent me to exercise the gifts He had given me to expose His plans. I could no longer compromise my position. Although it was painful, the call in me was cramped in that church that had become more of a compound than a haven of worship.

After suffering instead of submitting, I realized I needed to do it God's way. God convinced me serving was more significant. Once I began to surrender to serving, it became clear why stripping away the titles was important.

The power of becoming a servant as a leader became most prominent. I no longer came to be served but to serve. I searched for opportunities to serve others. In my search, I found predators that wanted me to serve their pockets. Out of those experiences, I learned to lean and depend solely on the Holy Spirit's guidance on where I was to serve. I no longer lived, but it was Christ that lived in me.

People have no problem following a leader that serves others instead of his desires. That's why Martin Luther King and Malcolm X had a great influence on those who followed them. They served.

Why would we fear the valley? Frankly, it's scary. We become open prey because of our fear.

We don't enjoy the pain that happens through valley experiences, but there are some things that come out of these necessary seasons that produce better outcomes or results because we went through them and not around them.

It's the pain that produces perfection. Not out of perfection strictly for excellence's sake in the immediate sense that we first consider, but out of perfecting or shaping our character in ways that gain God's approval.

Character building isn't for the fainthearted. There's a saying that I love to quote: "Iron sharpens iron,"[6] and when I quoted this in the past, a lot of people would cringe.

Now I cringe as I move to say it because I, through a lot of pain and agony, know what it feels like to experience the iron cutting across my flesh as though it were sharpening me. Iron going across iron yields extreme pain.

Yes, although painful, I still quote that saying because nothing produces a sharp sword better than another piece of iron. When you need to use a knife, you want it to be sharp and able to cut through what you need to cut through. There's nothing worse than a dull knife.

---

6. Proverbs 27:17.

It's the same with life. Dull knives won't do the job of cutting through or piercing into places that cause problems. Dull knives won't get you the solutions or answers to life's myriad of mounting messes that present themselves just because suffering is a byproduct of living.

You can't cut through the tough times that come into your life—whether it's hardships, pain, or suffering—if you don't have something sharp to cut through them.

Either you own the pain, or you learn to cut into it, making it fit into spaces that you design and/or desire to put it in. You are the creator of what this ought to be and not the pain itself.

I think it's worth plugging in right here an observation of how iron is made so that I can further clarify why this illustration is so powerful for us. Iron doesn't come out of the ground in the form that we see or hold in our hands as a knife. It must go through a process to produce its useful form.

> Iron ore is usually a mixture of iron and vast quantities of impurities such as sand and clay referred to as gangue. The iron found in iron ores are [*sic*] found in the form of iron oxides. As a result of these impurities, iron must be first separated from the gangue and then converted to pure iron. This is accomplished by the method of pyrometallurgy, a high-temperature process. The high temperatures are needed for the reduction of iron and the oxidation of the limestone.[7]

This is accomplished by placing the iron ore in a blast furnace.

7. "Iron Production," LibreTexts Chemistry, https://chem.libretexts.org/Courses/Tennessee_State_University/Inorganic_Chem_II_(CHEM4210)/04%3A_d-Block_Metal_Chemistry/4.01%3A_Properties_of_Transition_Metals/4.1.06%3A_Metallurgy/4.1.6.03%3A_The_Extraction_of_Iron/4.1.6.3.01%3A_Iron_Production.

"One of the most interesting parts of this redox reaction [in the blast furnace] is that the majority of the carbon dioxide formed is itself reduced when it comes into contact with the unburned coke"—not Coca-Cola but a fuel that is made from coal that is "derived from destructive distillation of low-ash, low-sulfur bituminous coal."[8] This procedure produces more reducing agents. As the process continues, the molten iron flows

> down through the furnace and collects at the bottom, where it is removed through an opening in the side. When it cools, the impure iron is brittle and in some cases soft due to the presence of the small impurities, such as sulfur and phosphorus.
>
> Thus, the impure iron coming from the bottom of the furnace is further purified. The most common method is the basic oxygen furnace. In the furnace, oxygen is blown into the impure iron. This is vital because the oxygen oxidizes the phosphorus and sulfur....
>
> The oxides either escape as gases or react with basic oxides that are added or used to line the furnace. This final purification step removes much of the impurities and the result is ordinary carbon steel. Thus iron is obtained through the process of oxidation-reduction.[9]

So, it is with our lives. We go into the furnace called "life." We go into it with a "blast." It initially doesn't look as if it's going to burn,

---

8. "How to Safely Recover Coke Dust?," *PrestiVac Blog*, prestivac.com/blog/how-to-safely-recover -coke-dust.

9. "Iron Production," LibreTexts Chemistry.

nor is it hot when we go into it. There's no intimidation by the process. Life, when we're young and just entering it, looks promising.

Then the blast of air is inserted through tests and trials. There's no heat yet. There's just a blast of air. Circumstances start to show that life is not exactly what you expected or wanted, but it's far from dismal at this point.

It's just disappointing. Maybe it's a little depressing. There's nothing that makes you want to throw in the towel, yet.

Then the furnace is turned on. It doesn't get hot at first. It takes a little time for you to feel the heat of your circumstances, but how quickly you feel the heat is based on your individual sensitivity to sudden changes in temperature.

If you're like me, I'm cold all of the time. They call that "cold-natured." I put on extra sweaters when other people are taking their shirts off. Those who are hot all of the time we consider to be "hot-natured."

Maybe you're "cold-natured" with life's circumstances. You can't take the cold so you can stand to have a little heat. So, you're okay with the furnace being turned on. You feel that you can handle it.

Maybe you're "hot-natured." When the heat is turned on in your world, you're ready to jump out of the furnace. "I can't take this anymore," you say. Or maybe you insist, "I give up—I don't deserve this." In your indignation, you may say, "Why did God allow this to happen to me?"

Is God the creator of this mess? Did He shape these shipwrecking circumstances? It may feel like it, or you may have been told that by others, but look again.

Who made the decisions? Who said that you had to do it this way? Was it you, your parents, or someone else? Was it you, them, or God? Make sure that you properly place blame on the real perpetrator.

It's easy to find fault with God. After all, He's the Creator, right? When you begin to blame God for the heat of the furnace, it seems that it gets hotter in the furnace. Now you *know* it's God.

You feel like you're a chicken in a deep fryer. Grease is popping all over the place in your life. It's one thing after the other. There's one evil turn of events after another until you feel hopeless. Life is no longer worth living.

The obstacles make you obstinate. Everything that comes out of your mouth is negative. You can't find the good in anything. Everything is sour. Everybody seems to have ulterior motives, and you are the victim.

"Great day in the morning—when will all of this stop?" is where you are in the process now. You're in the stage where the iron has been burned to the point where most of the impurities have burned away and evaporated like gas. The iron has fallen to the bottom.

You think you've been through the worst of it. You believe that surely things can't get any worse, but the process is far from over. There are still impurities in you that need to be burned out of you through the flame of the furnace to leave the purest form of iron. The purest life prepared for piercing through the challenges is yet to come. You need iron that has been purified to its final form in order for it to be useful for forming a weapon.

If you try to shape a weapon out of the original iron ore, you get a crumbled mess, but iron that goes through the fire twice makes a sturdy and reliable weapon.

Who allows pain to rule them? Many do. Unfortunately, they don't understand that the pain perfects what God has injected in them so that His purposes can be fulfilled through them. Without the pain of life's circumstances properly molded in the hands of God, their life lacks true meaning. Perceived success without meaning is no success at all.

We grapple with these seasons of testing and trouble that come our way. We'd rather avoid these times because they can be brutal and intense, pushing us to levels we didn't think were possible, but somehow, we get through them.

It's a good push, though. In these times, we find strength that we didn't know we had. We wonder that we are able to demonstrate this level of courage to face life's bumps in the road that we encounter.

But it's here in the valley that many times we find God. That's the iron-sharpening-iron moment we need. We may have known about Him—and even know Him in the purest sense—but we come to another level of knowing Him through seasons in the valley.

8

THE LIGHTHOUSE

You are the light of the world.
A city set on a hill cannot be hidden.

MATTHEW 5:14

walked in and there was silence. Her hands were dripping wet. She turned around to look at me with a very puzzled look on her face as I opened the bathroom door. There were questions in her gaze, but no words came out. I knew exactly how she felt.

I told her, "Slide your hands at an angle, and the dryer will come on." She still looked puzzled, as if to say, without a word spoken, "I already did that, I thought." So, I demonstrated for her what she needed to do. As I did, the lightbulb of her understanding came on.

Isn't it amazing that nothing comes with instructions anymore? Here she was, looking for some instructions on the machine as I walked in on her confusion. There were no directions, not even from the establishment that we were in, providing a clue as to how to use this new hand dryer made by Dyson. I guess the creators of things now intend to not pay to print out instructions anymore. They'd rather you go online to search for them instead. Or you have to find some gracious person who doesn't mind taking the time to show you how to use it.

They increase the price of the products but give you less in return. You open the box, and there's nothing in it but the product. Oh yeah, I forgot—there's the invoice inside, too. You call in to find out where the instructions are, and they tell you to go online to find them.

You end up having to jump down a bunny trail to get information. Some people give up and just choose not to use whatever product it is or return it to the maker. That's the life of many senior adults who are forced to come into the information age. Reluctantly, many choose to excuse themselves from looking like an idiot as they ask for help prowling the internet from some young whippersnapper.

Being pushed out of the process is aggravating at best. It's the same with cell phones. I can remember seeing my mother naturally navigate using her iPhone with ease, but most people her age cannot maneuver the updates and changes that are constantly made. So, they opt for the flip phone instead—if they can.

Even with instructions, most of us would prefer for someone to show us the way. That's called a practical application—a tried-and-true demonstration from someone who already knows how it works.

For the young who have grown up with technology all of their lives, the use of most new products is intuitive for them. Therefore, most times they don't refer to instructions. They open the product, plug it in, they play around with it for a few minutes, and before you know it, they've mastered the use of it.

That's easy-peasy, right? Those same young people believe that everything should work that way—including their lives. They don't need instructions. They don't need directions because they are the masters of their own destinies.

They've lived a few years, made a little money, and now they are the master teachers for everyone else. They even begin coaching others on how to live their best life.

They call themselves "influencers." They've mastered the show but not necessarily their messed-up lives that reflect neglect and excess. It's lights, camera, action. They live out their lives in front of their phone camera, posting and then reading the comments about their propped-up life. They're consumed with putting up appearances of glamour and glitz, all for the fame of it. They post images of extravagant lives on social media so that they get an extreme number of likes.

It's in the likes that they potentially gain a windfall from advertisers who want that audience. Is the show real or is it fake? Are the images reflective of a moment in time, or do their lives really look like this every day? Only they and God know, but my years tell me that they're anything but.

For those watching, it's everything. They're wrapped up in it. They base how they live, shop, and drive on what they see on social media. It causes many to become depressed because they can't seem to get an extreme makeover for their lives that even remotely resembles the pictures they see on Facebook, Instagram, or other social platforms.

If it's not depression, it's debt. In order to cash in on the life they want, they pile up debt in hopes of positioning themselves to get as many followers as possible so that they can live large, too.

Impostors. That's what they're called. The rented houses and cars are just props as they pose for the show, "The Rich and Wealthy."

Until their house of cards comes crashing down. Now it's crash and burn. Everything and everyone in their path become casualties.

How did they get here? They had all the answers. They wouldn't listen to Momma, Daddy, aunt or uncle, grandmother, or grandfather.

They knew everything, and when you know everything, those around you watching already know how it will end.

You told them the brick wall was up ahead, but they wouldn't listen. They call that hardheaded and going to the school of hard knocks. My mother used to say, "A hard head makes a soft behind." In other words, the *cost* of not listening to the voice of reason is a swift kick in the butt. It's pay me now or pay me later, but they will pay.

That's why the Word of God says that the old should teach the young. But the world tells the young that the old can't tell you anything about this life because they've never experienced it. What was done back then won't fit where they are today.

This couldn't be further from the truth. There is nothing new. As long as the earth revolves around the sun and day becomes night within twenty-four hours, life is full of trouble. Getting out of it requires experience.

It's in experiencing life, coupled with a love for our young people, that you pass on lessons learned. This requires those who are older to become very transparent, holding nothing back. Tell the truth. Don't just berate them. Tell them how you wore your dresses short when you were young, too. Tell them how you tried to smoke weed. Tell it all. Don't hold anything back.

Once you've exposed your past indiscretions and sins, tell them how Jesus saved you. It's important that they get the full picture. Don't just give the sordid details as you try to live vicariously through the young by recounting your escapades of days gone by. Remember, it was Jesus who met you at the point that you hit your own brick wall.

That's called being a light to the world. Jesus is the one that lit a light in you—not for you to hide it but for you to broadcast it. That's why it's important to be transparent about your past. In telling the stories, the transformation of who you have become lights the way for those still trapped in that way of life.

In Matthew 5:14–16, Jesus gave this assessment as He delivered the Sermon on the Mount:

> You are the light of the world. A city set on a hill cannot be hidden; nor do people light a lamp and put it under a basket, but on the lampstand, and it gives light to all who are in the house. Your light must shine before people in such a way that they may see your good works, and glorify your Father who is in heaven.

Don't be afraid of those that will judge you. This is a no-judgment zone where we are all set free from religious tyranny so that we help set others free. Don't stay in bondage. Get out of that mindset. It holds back the progress of the kingdom.

Religion says we're righteous, but Jesus is the one who took our place so that we can be *made* righteous through His sacrifice. We did nothing to earn our salvation. So, stop boasting. No one is righteous based on what they've done. We don't deserve what we've been given.

Yes, the Creator and Savior of the world washed their nasty, smelly feet. When they gave Him pushback, Jesus told them that if He didn't do it for them, they would not be part of what He was doing.

So, give up that narrative. It doesn't serve any of us, especially not Jesus. Telling that story is self-serving. Is that your objective?

That's part of the reason that the Church is in the mess it's in right now—self-righteousness and our rush to judgment. There's very little humility. Church leaders abuse those in the pew, seeking only those that will serve them.

Did you forget that Jesus washed the feet of His disciples? Yes, the Creator and Savior of the world washed their nasty, smelly feet. When they gave Him pushback, Jesus told them that if He didn't do it for them, they would not be part of what He was doing.

That goes for us today. We must lay down our lives and take up our cross. This requires listening and obeying the voice of God's Spirit only. Our will must be aligned with God's will. It must be more than just on the surface. This must be a complete change—from the inside out.

Jesus is looking for leaders that lead from their knees. It's the posture of humility, and it affirms who's in charge. He wants shepherds that have a heart like His—full of love. No more pomp and circumstance for men and women of the cloth and worship that's all about them. We are all equal. Wearing a title in the Lord's Church doesn't give you the power or the right to lord over those in the pew. None of us died to save anyone else—let alone get up out of the grave by our own power.

We can't draw the world by being their judge and jury. We draw them with love. We don't excuse sin, and we can't judge it either. Sin is determined to be so by God only. We don't write the law, and we are not His enforcers. Jesus does that.

Our job is to be witnesses of Jesus. What does that mean? It means that we give credible testimonial evidence that Jesus is who He says He is.

That's the view from the valley. It's a place that God brought us to with the intention that we learn who Jesus is. We gain a firsthand account of His deity because this is the very place where we experience His love and forgiveness.

Through this process, we become a lighthouse—a city set on a hill that cannot be hidden—and we give light to passersby who need direction. No longer seekers, we become givers.

It's through this journey that we witness Jesus as the Good Shepherd. Before we belonged to Him, He chose to save us. When we were His "frenemies," Christ died for us.

You know what frenemies are. They are people who pretend to love you, but they do everything they can to hurt you. They go out of their way to hook up with others who really don't like you to connive and contrive your demise.

That's what the Pharisees did to Jesus. In public, they were as curious as everyone else, but secretly, they were seeking ways to undermine His ministry. They thought their muscle was in their tricks to trip up Jesus. The mission was to get Him to contradict God's Word. Every miracle became a spectacle, but not everyone worshipped the Miracle Worker.

"How dare He?" That was their response when Jesus healed on the Sabbath. Now they've got Him right where they want Him—hook, line, and sinker. This will surely bring Him down, leaving Him crawling and begging for their forgiveness. After all, they were chief in the temple—not Him.

They sat in the seat of judgment, dressed in their liturgical vestments, tapered to fit their taunting threats. They didn't know who He was. Surely, they had Him in their grips now, and they went for broke.

Jesus told the man with the withered hand in Mark 3:1–6 to stand up in front of everyone and then proceeded to ask a question. In verse 4, He asked a pointed legal question of the learned that were watching: "Is it lawful to do good on the Sabbath or to do harm, to save a life or to kill?" They said nothing, but I'm sure fumes were exuding from the tops of their heads. They were furious.

So, instead of addressing the elephant in the room drawn by the religious elite, Jesus turned to the man and told him to "stretch out your hand." When the man obeyed, he was healed. This sent the Pharisees reeling with anger and began their quest to find others who wanted to kill Jesus, too.

These are the types of vultures and wild beasts that we were saved from when we met Jesus in the valley. We got to see Him, firsthand, take His rod and slay those enemies that wanted to take away our newfound freedom brought about through Christ.

With one fell swoop, He shut them down by doing what only He can do. He healed. He forgave us. He loved us. He saved us.

9

DRIVE

*So the watchman reported, saying, "He went up to them
and is not coming back; and the driving is like the driving
of Jehu the son of Nimshi, for he drives furiously!"*

2 KINGS 9:20 NKJV

or forty-two months, I was in the wilderness. A dry place. It
appeared that I couldn't win for losing. Everything and everyone
that I held dear to me was gone—whether physically or mentally.

Except God. God used those forty-two months to train and equip
me to be a voice for Him.

What does that mean? A voice for Him? Many times, for me, it
meant that I looked ridiculous. Some family members just put up
with me, not knowing whether they should embrace, tolerate, or
ostracize me because of who I had become.

For roughly 1,260 days, I lay in weight, waiting for God to move
on many of the consistent words that He had given me to prophesy
because of a vision that He had given me.

Yes…I meant I lay in *weight*. There is a weight that is clear when
you wait on God. The weight of the wait. The weight is those things
that lie in the balance. We judge those things and make decisions on

111

how to move as we wait. Those things shape our thinking and our future based on the importance we place on—or how we weigh— the various obstacles that appear before us and how we act on them. I believed that I was waiting on God, but God was waiting on me.

What was He waiting on me for? He was waiting on me to see the truth of the matter and to act on it. That's the weight that I was struggling with. What was the truth He was waiting for me to see?

The glaring truth was that my life reflected the many *shades of redemption*. The tangled web of my life over the prior ten to fifteen years was a product of pain and suffering, which was no different than what anyone else may have to endure. But what I chose to do in response to that pain and suffering was what God wanted to see. What He wanted for me singled me out from the crowd. He wanted me to be in this world, but not of it.

God was waiting for me to finish writing these books that He stored up in me. He always delivers His messages through human beings. That didn't change because I was reluctant to participate. My life would've remained stagnant had I not obeyed Him.

My choices mattered—in every aspect and scope of analysis that could be wrought. Was I waiting for God to make the choice for me? I don't think so. I believe I was waiting for God to change His mind about the matter. I was waiting for God to say, "You don't have to go through this. I know you're right. He was wrong, so go on with your life as you see fit." This never happened. God never agreed with my sentiments. Instead, He waited. Patiently. For forty-two months.

Instead, as life poured out its river of circumstances, I began to change. As I grew as a person, I began to see that my choices were lining up with what God originally intended for me.

Choosing to forgive and take my husband back—at the moment that he asked and returned—is what God asked me to do. But He left the option for me not to accept the challenge, with all of the pain caused by what I knew to be the facts surrounding my ex-husband's affairs and actions both during and after the marriage ended. The choice was still mine to make—alone.

I had every right, based on God's own law, to remarry and move into another life as I saw fit. But choosing to do so would have meant what for me?

Would this offer the life that I *really* wanted? What did I want? I wanted the life that God wanted for me. He knows and sees what I can't. Why would I continue to question that truth if I believed what and in whom I said I believed?

Even in light of the so-called facts, which God called smoke and mirrors, why would I want my ex-husband back? After all the pain and suffering he caused me? He flaunted his girlfriend in front of me, our children, and my friends as though we meant nothing to him. Our marriage and commitment of over twenty-plus years meant absolutely nothing to him. Did I want to go through that level of pain again? Absolutely not!

The Spirit of God, in the forty-two months that we shared together, shed a lot of light on who I am in light of who He is. He told me, "Don't forget—I chose you first. You didn't choose Me. Although you were raised to love Me because of the family you were born into, you were still born in and shaped in sin, and that sin separates you from Me. Just as Michael needs My forgiveness, so do you. I want you to be a human expression of how I love. I promise—the *day* you ask, I will accept you, forgive you, love you, and bring you into My family—without question—and when you do these same acts of loving-kindness, you represent Me in the flesh. When you do this, you prove that you are Mine."

I realized—my choice was no choice at all. To obey God in this was just as much for me as it was for my ex. It's true, there were some selfish motives here. We all have tendencies to look out for ourselves first. That's the *tangled web.*

My obedience would bring redemption for my ex that may or may not have ever presented itself again like this otherwise, but it was also redemption for me. Without this level of obedience, the forgiveness that I was seeking in my own personal relationship with God was on the line—just as it was for him.

This charge to obey became a necessary pain. A necessary evil pill that I willfully swallowed and accepted because I needed to be healed in this area. The light bulb came on for me about my own need for God's forgiveness and redemption.

I had to cast off the self-righteous indignation that rose up in me because it was an offense that caused me to have things in common with that evil, twisting spirit of Leviathan. And I wanted no part in him. This was the very thing that would keep me, if I allowed it to fester in my thought process, from the freedom offered when I accepted Jesus Christ as my Savior.

This type of indignation says, "You're right. You're the one that's righteous—not them. They did you wrong. You're better than them. You've never done anything as bad as that." But God's Word says, "All have sinned and fall short of the glory of God" (Romans 3:23 NIV). *All* includes me—with my self-righteous self.

You are not judged by the problems that you face but by how you face them. God never promised that your life would be pain-free or that there would be less pain because you chose to live for Him. The truth is that whether you choose to live for God or not, you will suffer. That's a guarantee. You can cash that check at the bank.

But there are benefits to suffering *with* Christ. The operative word here is *with*. When you suffer after choosing to live for Christ, He chooses to suffer with you. He gets in "the boat" of your life's circumstances, and instead of you having to row the boat—feeling the weight of the oars and the difficulty in lifting them as well as finding the strength to push through the waves of water crashing against you as you dash ahead in life in order to get you from point A to point B—He rows with you.

He takes the oars from you and tells you to rest in Him while He rows the boat for you. He says, "Take My yoke upon you, and learn of Me; for I am meek and lowly in heart: and ye shall find rest unto your souls" (Matthew 11:29 kjv).

Through your faith in Him, you enlist the same resurrection power that raised Christ from the dead, and you become empowered to overcome every situation or obstacle that comes against you and God's purposes for your life. Knowing the end from the beginning, He inserts Himself in time to change your outcomes.

It is through the finished work of the cross that He interjects salvation—not just in eternity, but right now and for all time. What He did on the cross went into the future to make all things work according to His plan of salvation.

That means He saw your problem with your son sitting in jail for a crime he didn't commit, and He went from the cross to that jail cell—years into the future, standing in the gap, even causing you to pray for him.

He knew how and why it would happen. He knew that your son would curse God and you, but still God planned to make a way out for him. He did it before you prayed, and even if you didn't pray for him, God wouldn't let an unwilling heart stand between Him and your son.

He always comes in the nick of time. Yes, He paid for every minor or major detail that causes us to stray away from Him with only one motivation in His mind—*love*.

That love won't quit. It won't let go. It holds on until you grab on. It weathers every storm or turbulent event that comes or goes.

It moves mountains. It slays dragons. It defeats every enemy. It never loses a battle.

Love endures. It passes the test of time. It creates and recreates itself through its own efforts. And don't confuse things—God is; therefore, love is—period. That's the end of the subject.

Love endures. It passes the test of time. It creates and recreates itself through its own efforts.

This type of love is better than I deserve—let alone my ex. Then, why can't I freely dispense this same kind of love to someone who has betrayed me openly? To someone who pierced me deep into my soul—whether with willful intent to harm me or not—I now realize I have an obligation to give this type of love voluntarily, especially when it hurts so intensely.

How does the Church get to participate in this? Remember the dream? The Church is hiding, too. We're all not driving—stagnant, shaken, and not able to move.

Much of this story initiates with the dilemma surrounding human suffering. From the beginning of time, humans have shared this common thread. No matter what our social or financial status, cultural background, or pedigree, we all, at some point or another, will endure suffering. Some of us will endure more than others.

Whether it's health concerns, poverty, betrayal, or deep wounds from life's losses, we somehow endure it. There's a Scripture in Romans 8:18 that states: "For I reckon that the sufferings of this present time are not worthy to be compared with the glory which shall be revealed in us" (KJV). The glory—that's what everybody's talking about. What is "the glory," and why does it need to be revealed?

The glory is God's essence that pours out over the world because of His unwavering, never-ending, always pursuing love for us—whether we acknowledge Him or not or whether we believe in Him or not. Glory is who He is. There's no glory on earth without Him.

But how can the glory be revealed in us when there's so much pain from our suffering? How do we get beyond all the pain as it piles up—an inch at a time—until all we and the world see is the resulting agony of it all?

It is when our faith in Him is demonstrated through our actions and God responds to it in kind that God's glory increases on the earth. Faith activates God's glory.

The glory is revealed when the power of Christ's resurrection is manifested in the way we overcome. It's not just because we get through but that we don't look like the tough times that we've come through. That's a testimony. Getting beyond the tough times despite the suffering brings about endurance. Revelation 12:11 states: "They conquered him by the blood of the Lamb and by the word of their testimony, for they did not love their lives in the face of death" (HCSB).

Whom did they conquer? Satan and his angels are who the author, John, is talking about in this Scripture.

You may ask, "But how do we accomplish this?" I'm so glad you asked. That is the purpose of this book: to share insights downloaded to me from the person of the Holy Spirit that is alive in me.

He allowed a specific set of circumstances in my life that caused one painful event after another until there was a pileup of betrayals, losses, pain, and hurt where my life looked more like a crime scene than a green pasture, as some want to tell you is the life of a saint. I'm here to tell you that if your life shows shadows of heartache, health issues, disappointments, or betrayals, you can still be counted among those known as saints.

Our faith in His love and promises defies all the odds stacked against us. His promises are more important than the facts of a matter. Yes, the doctor says you have cancer, but your faith says that by His stripes you are healed. You stand firm in that knowledge of the truth—unwavering—no matter what it looks like with the test results or the doctor's facts.

That's where you stand in the face of the facts. Herein lies evidence of the truth that we believe in. Thereby, faith is activated and mobilized to fight for us.

In the end, truth speaks volumes and breaks us away from this same beaten pathway of the lackluster life that says we can't be healed. For whether it is in this life or the life to come, we are healed because of His stripes. So, whether the doctor declares that we are cancer-free or we succumb to the woes of cancer's sting, we confidently proclaim, "Death, where is your sting?" He conquered death and the grave so that we live eternally with Him. Whether we live or die, we win.

Faith in this truth gives us power—power to stand in the face of adversity and say *no*, I won't go without a fight. And so, we stand and fight.

The topic in this chapter deals with the many shades of redemption. Has the Church become so shallow that we don't see hopelessness all around us? Is it that we don't see, or we don't want to see? We'd prefer that someone else handle certain things. Sound familiar? How are we like Jonah?

One way is our approach to abortion rights. We all know that this is not pleasing to God, but neither is telling lies. I don't hear anyone preaching, "All liars will have their part in the lake that burns." Have you? Or you hear of so-called Christians who killed a doctor who performed abortions. Which is the greater sin? Neither. Both are wrong in God's sight.

Is it just our attempt to stand up for something or are we really wanting the greater good? If we want to do good, why don't we see churches that reach out in love, not judgment, to young women who find themselves in a place of an unwanted pregnancy? Jesus said that they will know us by our love—not by a judge's robe that many of us wear. God wants us to show mercy to those who feel they have no other way out.

When it comes to one of America's greatest sins, slavery, no one wants to talk about it. Reparations? The first thing said is, "Those were my ancestors, not me." But did you benefit from your ancestors' choices? Has your life received benefits or privileges from your white skin that haven't been afforded to my black skin? If you require every other crime to be punishable by prison time or monetary penalties, why has there not been anything offered and implemented for descendants of slaves? I don't see anyone preaching about that except those who were once enslaved.

Another atrocity is those from the pulpit claiming political office seekers as God's chosen even though there's no fruit on their tree to prove their claims. It's an abuse of power when men and women of the cloth influence those who follow them. It's an example of leading the sheep to slaughter.

The Church is the most segregated of all institutions today. Why is that? I understand that most people worship with their families, but ministry leadership must thoughtfully seek opportunities to at minimum fellowship with congregations of another race to broaden their sphere of influence at the local level.

We run from discussing sins that need to be stopped immediately, but we don't make efforts to stop them. No one except the victim stands up for the number of children who have been molested by men of the cloth—whether it be priests, pastors, bishops, or other congregants. It's abhorrent. Yet we sit silently, waiting for the justice system to step in. Or we want the victims to stand up for themselves, but by the time they are able to stand up against the predators that accosted them, the statute of limitations is up.

Specifically, Jonah was called to go beyond his borders to preach repentance to people he didn't like. Today, the mandate is the same, but we must view the process as God does. The people who need the message of repentance the most are not outside our borders. They are our neighbors. They are our children. They are young girls who become prostitutes, right in our backyards. Young men resort to alternate sources of earning an income because going to school didn't work for them, and they want to live the "baller's" lifestyle.

These issues and more are what we face today. We can no longer be silent, and we won't see the defeat of the enemy as long as we're divided. United we stand. Divided we fall.

10

THE CHASE

*"The chase only matters when
you're afraid of being caught."*

You always told me to stay off the freeway."

"Yes, that's true."

"You said it was suicide."

"Then let us hope I was wrong." These are the infamous statements between Morpheus and Trinity from the sci-fi action film *The Matrix Reloaded*, which was the second sequel in the *Matrix* trilogy.

I don't know about you, but I didn't want to watch this film at first. In fact, when it came to theaters, I refused to go although I enjoyed the first *Matrix* movie. I'm usually opposed to how Hollywood would rather play off of the hype of previous blockbuster films than create new movie themes worthy of watching. To me, it shows a lack of creativity.

I happened to watch it, though, when we were invited to some friend's house one evening and it was already on. I wasn't going to object to watching it since it was already on, and it wasn't my house.

Wouldn't you know that I got caught up in the storyline anyway? I'm not much of a fan of sci-fi, but there was something different for me about this film. I instantly picked up on spiritual messages or connotations all the way through the content of the movie. My children say that I can do that with any movie, including *Bambi*. Hahaha!

Yes, it's true to its sci-fi genre, but if you look closely, you can hear ties to the spiritual—just to start with, in the choice of the characters' names. The city is called Zion, and the cast of characters is in a tug of war between opposing forces to save both Zion and the Keymaker.

At the point that the car chase happens, Morpheus and Trinity have successfully rescued the Keymaker from the Merovingian, the demon-possessed, villainous perpetrator of all the evil deeds done in the city. They are able to pull this off as a consequence of his scorned wife's need for revenge.

The Merovingian's wife watches as her husband talks about a beautiful, young woman sitting across the restaurant. He tells how he causes her to come under his spell after she eats the dessert that he's poisoned with a mind-altering chemical. The camera view switches back and forth from him to this woman as she comes under his spell and has to get up to go to the ladies' bathroom, which the Merovingian already knows will happen. As she exits, so does he without apology.

In his bold and brazen demonstration in front of his now-incensed wife, he's left himself open to her brutal attacks from her abandoned emotional state. She just wants life to go back to the way it was between them before they came to the city, but she also will not be outdone by the Merovingian as he publicly disgraces her.

It's her idea to turn the Keymaker over to Morpheus and Trinity, and she doesn't care who knows it. As they leave with the Keymaker,

Morpheus and Trinity are spotted by the Twins, who are the evil, conspiring cohorts of the Merovingian. They demand the release of the Keymaker, and at the sight of the Twins, the Keymaker decides that he'd be better off without help.

Running for his life, the Keymaker happens upon a car that he's able to unlock and start. Enigmatically, he supposes that he'll make a clean getaway, but Trinity realizes what he's up to, and she opens the driver's door, telling him to get in the back seat. He doesn't understand that he doesn't stand a chance of surviving or getting away from the Twins without their help. It doesn't stop him from trying, for after all, he's the Keymaker, and he has keys that can open just about anything.

Thereby, the chase between the opposing forces ensues. It reminded me of Pharoah chasing after the children of Israel. Once the dust settled and the initial grieving was over, the Egyptians realized there was no one capable of doing the work the children of Israel once did—therefore, the chase.

God knew that Pharoah would come after the children of Israel because He hardened his heart. There had to be a supernatural reason for the children of Israel to commit to God. It wasn't just the parting of the Red Sea or walking on dry land that made them love God. It was seeing their enemies drown in that same sea that led to their salvation.

What about us? What or who's chasing us? We all have enemies, whether we realize it or not. How do we deal with them?

In my dream of being in a car surrounded by shooters, I didn't even know who the gunmen were who were shooting at me, but they obviously were my enemies. That's how it is. It looks like your cousin Sarah has it in for you because she's always cutting you down, but it's not Sarah. There are forces working through Sarah that want to hurt you. Those forces are your *real* enemy.

Stop fighting with Sarah. Jesus tells us to love our enemies. He tells us in Matthew 5:44 (KJV) "But I say unto you, love your enemies, bless them that curse you, do good to them that hate you, and pray for them which despitefully use you, and persecute you." Don't even claim that you're waging war against the demons working through Sarah. We don't chase demons.

How do you fight an unseen enemy? You know he's there. You feel the tug-of-war struggle, but you appear to be struggling against people, not Satan.

Don't ever tell anyone—not even yourself—that you're chasing demons. Why would you need to chase defeated foes? You certainly don't need to fight what Jesus has already successfully overcome and continues to overcome on your behalf.

It's called spiritual warfare, but it's not your typical war. Ephesians 6:12 states, "For our struggle is not against flesh and blood, but against the rulers, against the powers, against the world forces of this darkness, against the spiritual forces of wickedness in the heavenly places."

What exactly is spiritual warfare? It is the ongoing fight between the followers of Christ and the followers of Satan, and the battlefield is in our minds.

How do you fight an unseen enemy? You know he's there. You feel the tug-of-war struggle, but you appear to be struggling against people, not Satan. That's how cowards fight. They put other people up to do their dirty work. They throw the rock and then hide.

But this adversary was defeated by Jesus when He conquered death and the grave by getting up out of it. The truth of His Spirit living in us terrifies Satan because Satan knows the power it holds.

The power of what Jesus did on the cross not only took care of those things that came before His death, but it also went into the future, including every situation that we will ever face—into all eternity. "The Son of God appeared for this purpose, to *destroy the works of the devil*" (1 John 3:8).[10] When Jesus said it was finished, He meant everything. What we must do is stand. We must persevere through those things that look like terrorism but are actually only smoke and mirrors.

They can only threaten. They can't kill you. They don't have the legal right to. Jesus took care of that.

Second Corinthians 10:3–5 (KJV) explains it this way:

For though we walk in the flesh, we do not war after the flesh: (For the weapons of our warfare are not carnal, but mighty through God to the pulling down of strong holds;) Casting down imaginations, and every high thing that exalteth itself against the knowledge of God, and bringing into captivity every thought to the obedience of Christ.

This type of fight requires us to know who we are. We can't fake it on this battlefield. We must be certain of the truth: that Jesus is our Savior, and the same power that resurrected Him from the grave is at work within us.

Sit with that truth for a moment. The power that caused Jesus to go from death to life, which is the reverse of the natural order of humanity, is not just available to us but is at work in us.

---

10. Emphasis added.

I know. That's a lot. It's heavy and overwhelming all at the same time, but it's true, and we must be assured of it. If you're not sure, Satan and his imps will run over you.

This reminds me of a dream I had back in 2012, in which my former husband and I entered a church that seemed very familiar, but there was no name on the outside of the building. We entered a very large vestibule or lobby area, and oddly, it was substantial in size. It could easily accommodate two hundred people.

As we walked in, a person ran past us. We tried to stop him to ask the man a question, but he wouldn't stop. He had a look of sheer fear on his face. Then there were three or four more people who ran past us, screaming and looking for a place to hide.

We proceeded to walk through the lobby to the entrance to the sanctuary. We opened two very tall and wide double doors. I could see through the windows of the church that there were dark clouds hovering over the church, and there was slightly dim lighting in the sanctuary. But I was consumed by all of the people running scared all throughout the building.

By this time, I noticed that my former husband, who had come into the building with me, had run away as well in total fear. They were all afraid, but what or who had them running around the building in total fear? It was helter-skelter. They were running like chickens with their heads chopped off.

I started walking toward the front of the sanctuary. I noticed the upholstered pews and plush carpeted floors. This place felt comfortable. It felt like home to me.

I just couldn't understand what all of the commotion was about. What had just happened?

The altar area was adorned with fresh flowers just at the foot of the lectern. The podium had plush upholstered high-back chairs, and the choir stand had ample seating. Just as I noticed the instruments, I decided to sit down on one of the pews near the center of the sanctuary. I picked up a songbook, but all the while, I saw through my peripheral vision people continuing to run, screaming and trying to find a place to hide.

If everyone else was afraid, why was I not? I flipped through the songbook, reminiscing about the songs we sang when I was a child. Then a handsome man walked up to me.

"Do you think it is going to rain?" he asked. "I don't know, but it looks like it's going to," was my answer.

We engaged in conversation for quite a while. He had a striking presence, an infectious smile, and a commanding voice. I was drawn to him because of his corny humor, and it felt as if I already knew him. I became comfortable around him, although I still saw people running, trying to find a safe place to hide.

Then I asked him, "Why is everyone running in fear?" He said, "I don't know."

What I hadn't paid attention to was that his appearance and demeanor had begun to change. He went from being a strikingly handsome man to one who had a dark shadow over him that was concerning.

Despite the changes in his appearance, I continued holding a conversation with him. As we continued, his presence became very dark and dangerous. Now fear began to set in.

As fear crept in, I realized that he was the reason everyone was so afraid. I tried to hide my fear, but the changes in him became so grotesque I could hardly breathe. Yet, we continued the conversation. I didn't want to let on that I was afraid or intimidated by his presence. I was not going to run in fear of him. He picked up on my knowledge of who he was, and he pointed to the floor.

"Can you pick up that gun that's on the floor?" he asked. My heart was now so gripped with fear, and I could feel every beat of it, but I had to try to keep him at bay. As I bent my knees to get the gun from the floor, I refused to take my eyes off of him because I didn't trust him. But for one split second, I looked away because I couldn't get a grip on the gun. As I pulled the gun up, he pulled a machete out from behind him. At that moment, I woke up, and I heard the Spirit of God say, "You don't entertain demons. You cast them out."

The Word in 1 Peter 5:8 says Satan is *like* a roaring lion. He's not a lion. He wants to be *seen* as a lion—perceived as a threat. He's seeking someone to take out. That is why we stand firm on the truth of Jesus. It is in Him that we have the victory.

This assurance that we have is not cockiness. It's confidence—not in ourselves but in Jesus. We "overcame him by the blood of the Lamb, and by the word of their [our] testimony" (Revelation 12:11 KJV).

Because the battleground is in our minds, we must take our thoughts captive. Why is that, we may ask? Because if we don't, Satan will. That's why this spiritual warfare is different.

You take your thoughts captive by what you believe. Don't let those negative words spoken become your truth. Don't allow anyone to speak negatively about you when God speaks so highly of you. His thoughts of you are good, and so are His plans for you.

To accomplish this, decree what God says from His Word about you. Job 22:28 (KJV) says, "Decree a thing, and it shall be established unto thee: and the light shall shine upon thy ways."

It's not just vain repetition. You're changing not just your mind but the outcome in a way that everyone around you will see because your heart has changed who you are.

For example, Ephesians 2:10 states, "For we are His workmanship, created in Christ Jesus for good works, which God prepared beforehand so that we would walk in them." Now, turning this Scripture into a decree sounds like this: "For *I am* God's workmanship, created for such a time as this through Jesus the Christ for every good work assigned to me, and I will walk in them." Are you picking up what I'm laying down?

Anytime we begin a statement with "I am," we partner with the Great I AM, God the Father, to accomplish the rest of the sentence. So, no more statements of "I am broke," or "I am sick." No. It's "I am healed by the stripes of Jesus," and "I am everything that God says I am."

When you decree these things, you must believe that they are true. No wavering. Even if the doctors have given up hope, hold on to hope, even in the face of death.

Even death can't keep us from the promises of God. First Corinthians 15:55–57 (KJV) says, "O death, where is thy sting? O grave, where is thy victory? The sting of death is sin; and the strength of sin is the law. But thanks be to God, which giveth us the victory through our Lord Jesus Christ." Jesus swallowed up the sting of death because in death, we are eternally healed and will live with Jesus forever—never to die again.

You're short on cash? Decree: "My God will supply all of my needs according to His riches in glory." You're not asking for riches. You're asking for your needs to be fulfilled by our rich God. There's a difference.

Spiritual warfare is an art, not a science. God uses our unique set of circumstances—education, family, and financial predicament—to move us to pray for people, places, and things. Just as soldiers each have their own assignments, so do we. As such, our Commander in Chief, Jesus, and His five-star General, the Holy Spirit, assign us to the posts where we need to be. That's why we must stay sensitive to hear what the Spirit of God is leading us to do and pray for. There's no room for renegades.

In this army, renegades don't become heroes. They get slaughtered. You can't slay the dragon that you can't see with your physical eyes. You have to use your spiritual eyes to see. That's only possible when the Holy Spirit is your General. So, submit to His authority, and you will ultimately win.

It is also important to connect with a prayer ministry that's equipped to sharpen what the Holy Spirit is leading you to do. We must all submit to someone, but who you submit to needs to be led by the Holy Spirit. Ask Him who you should connect with. Don't be anxious or feel obligated to only connect with the church you're a member of. God is bigger than that, and He has prayer warriors all over the world that are praying without ceasing. They are fully aligned with God's will, and He knows them personally. He wants you to be a part of a community of believers and equipped. Therefore, He will guide you to where you need to land.

Don't be afraid of the weapons that form against you—not even the bullets. The weapons of life may form, but they come to build your own arsenal so that you are equipped to fight back.

You can't effectively fight an enemy you don't know. Don't be afraid to know who you're fighting. It changes your perspective on what works, and you find that fighting with eyes of flesh causes you to lose. You must look at the fight through spiritual eyes and know you are not alone in this fight.

Just as the Keymaker in *The Matrix Reloaded* can make keys to unlock any door, Jesus has given us keys to unlock the kingdom of heaven. It's high time that we used them.

11

KEEP GOING

*But as for you, be strong and **do not give up**,*
for your work will be rewarded.

2 CHRONICLES 15:7 (NIV)

I love coffee. I can't tell you the joy it brings to my morning. From the smell of it brewing to the very last sip from my cup, I'm enamored.

Don't get me wrong—I'm not one of those people who are sour first thing in the morning and can only get it together after drinking their first cup. No, I'm quite the opposite. I am a morning person, but coffee that's brewed to perfection seals the day for me.

I was introduced to coffee at a young age by our mother. She drank it religiously and sometimes by the potful. We just didn't know that our mother was giving us cream—no coffee—but we would sit, coffee cup in hand, celebrating the morning moments with her as if we were really relishing the taste of fresh-brewed coffee. Boy, the imagination of children is amazing, isn't it?

As a teenager, I became very invested in healthy living and thought the caffeine found in coffee was harmful to our bodies. So, for many years, I didn't drink coffee, and in fact, I talked down to people who drank it.

Until I turned fifty. I needed to lose weight, and I bought and read so many books on weight loss, including the book, *Eat Right for Your Type*. This book mentioned that a small amount of coffee was good for digestion.

I took my first sip, and I was hooked. How did I make it all those years without my coffee fix? Inquiring minds wanted to know, what was all the hoopla about?

Early on, my interest was more about my mother. I thought she was amazing. She was beautiful and intelligent. She was accomplished, but you wouldn't know it because she was unassuming. I don't know why my brothers and sister longed for a cup of joe, but my young mind assumed that if she drank coffee, it must be something I wanted to do.

For most of my life, I lived in my mother's shadow. I thought that I never measured up to her. She was as beautiful inside as she was on the outside—a genuine heart to the core and always saw the good in people, even if they only showed the worst parts of themselves.

She was the Energizer Bunny. She worked all the time. Even in her idle time, she was reading, writing, studying, calling to encourage, or cleaning something. Until she was diagnosed with pancreatic cancer.

Almost as soon as she heard the word *cancer*, she believed it was her end. We were all frantic. We went with her from one doctor to another, then to specialists, only to hear them say there was nothing that they could do for her.

She looked at death without fear of it, but we weren't ready to let go. Even as we watched her weight dwindle and she became frail in a matter of four months, we refused to give up hope.

It's hope that keeps us going—the hope of a brighter tomorrow. We have hope for a better future because our children's determination to be change agents convinces us that it's possible.

When the attacks of life hit hard, where do you find hope? Do you look for it in politicians? Do you look for it in your job, profession, or money? Do you try going to church to find it?

You're up to your eyeballs in debt. You're living paycheck to paycheck, and now you've lost your job. You were already robbing Peter to pay Paul. Where's that hope now?

He told you that he would love you forever, but three children in and after twenty years of marriage, he's moved out with his new girlfriend. You feel like your heart is that lump in your throat, and you can't move. Broken is an understatement. Hope? What is that?

It was Grandma's hands that cooked your meals, changed your diapers, and spanked your behind when you got in trouble. Now Grandma's hands begin to lose the life in them as she drifts off to sleep, never to wake up again. "She's gone," they say. Motionless, you try to muster the strength to believe that your life will go on. Hope seems lost at this point.

My life was like a sad blues song that was
playing on repeat. It was as if someone
took a baseball bat, hitting me at the knees
and knocking the wind out of me.

Could your fate be sealed by these occurrences? When my life seemed to shatter, I couldn't breathe. My life was like a sad blues song that was playing on repeat. It was as if someone took a baseball bat, hitting me at the knees and knocking the wind out of me.

There was no medicine that I could take to cure the pain I felt. It was rolling down like hills and valleys through my mind with memories of a past that I longed to replay. How did this happen?

It became the wilderness for me—an inescapable prison cell that became my classroom. Some of my greatest lessons were learned during that season of my life.

I became a student of pain. Initially, I made my home there. It was uncomfortable and unbearable.

One day, I said to myself, "If I dwell here too long, I'll take up residence. I will not make my home in a potful of spoiled meat and wilted produce."

Every day, the Holy Spirit comforted me. He was the best friend you could ever have. He sat with me, and I mean that in the physical sense of the word. I felt His presence sit with me—like old friends that have known you all your life. They know all the sordid details of all the ups and downs. They know you, and you know that they love you. You trust them with your hurt and the details of what brought you pain.

That's what I was waiting on while sitting in the car in my dream. It wasn't what, but whom. The Holy Spirit had to step in to complete my process of preparation. The enemy didn't want me to become fully prepared to face him because he understands the power that we possess when we know who we are—and more importantly, when we know who he is. Therefore, he brought out the "big guns" to attack me on every side.

The bullets being shot at me were meant to at least stop my assignment, and the shooters would've loved to kill me, but God wouldn't let them. By showing me what was to come, God wanted me to look beyond the problems to see His promises and rest in them while I completed the assignments that I had to complete.

Instead, I wrestled with the problems for way too long. But once I gained perspective, I proceeded to drive off from what I thought was a CSI scene. Those problems no longer had me in the grip of fear.

The pain subsided gradually until it no longer mattered what anybody was doing—not my ex-husband, my son's episodes of mental insanity, or my other children's denial of God's existence. No. Nothing and no one would stop me anymore.

The fight changed. I began fighting like I'd already won. This is a divine strategy that the Holy Spirit infused in me to get me in a position to move ahead with power.

You can't fight an enemy when you don't understand how they fight. You need proven strategies that work, and the only way to do that is to follow the Holy Spirit's directions. He knows whom we're fighting because Satan is His enemy, too.

That's the reason, I believe, that the Holy Spirit chose to take up the challenge of finishing my boot camp. I needed to learn how to depend solely on and hear from Him as I worked the strategies as He gave them to me.

I've always had a strong sense of discernment, but the Holy Spirit worked to help hone those skills so that I became keenly aware of exactly what He wanted me to do in every circumstance—even down to the smallest details that you would think are too insignificant for God to care about, but He did. He used every moment as a teachable moment so that nothing was wasted.

You can't develop these types of skills without going through the trial-and-error period. I made a lot of mistakes. I thought I was hearing the Holy Spirit tell me specific dates, but I would be off—or He wasn't conveying a specific timeframe at all. I had to learn to wait for all the details and not assume what He was saying.

Sometimes, in my eagerness to deliver messages, I got it wrong. Haste always makes waste, but the Holy Spirit didn't scold or waste any of my failures. Making mistakes was important to the process.

These blunders taught me to wait on Him to give me all the details, without assumptions. My setbacks became His successes in training and developing me as a weapon.

I had a lot of ego, so Holy Spirit had a big job helping me to let go of it. It couldn't be about me. That need that I have to always be right had to go as well, because if God tells me to deliver a message that He later chooses to change because of a repentant heart that received the message, who am I to stand in His way?

Even this writing is a labor of love—not from me but from God. He wouldn't let this go. He intended for me to labor over this work, hashing out the details of every deliverance that He rendered on my behalf during the trials and turmoil sent my way to take me out, in order for you to know how to maneuver through the truckload of troubles that are sent your way.

He wanted it to go down to the tiniest of facts so that you have measurable steps to follow. He wanted this material to be a working tool that shapes and sharpens your spiritual weapons in a safe and secure manner.

He doesn't mind you messing up but doesn't want you to give up. That's not an option. You must know that you're not in this alone. He's with you every step of the way. Just tell Him your areas of weakness. Confess what challenges you, and He'll step in to give you what you need. So, don't give up when it gets tough. Winners never quit, and quitters never win. His ultimate goal for you is that you keep going because He knows that you're already a winner—even in your perceived failure.

We all prefer winners. We don't want to hang out with losers. But everything's not what it seems. Many times, what looks successful isn't at all. Success is not always measured by what you can see but by what you can't see. When I worked at the bank, we had a customer who came into the bank every week with old overalls on and drove an old pickup truck. Based on what we could see, he was far from a success, but he was a longtime customer of mine, and I knew what he had.

He once told me, "You shouldn't wear your money. Money needs to make money, and it can't do that when you're wearing it. That doesn't give much of a return except in greedy friends."

So, don't get caught up in how things look. Appearances can deceive you if all you see is what's on the surface. Look deeper. When you can't see beyond the smoke and mirrors, ask for help from the Holy Spirit. You need spiritual eyes to see.

That brings me to the final piece in my first dream. The Church, too, is waiting for a move of God like no other. It can only come when we are fully equipped like soldiers with the Holy Spirit.

We are moving into a time when we must be sharpened like weapons. We must be vigilant and painfully aware of what's going on around us. There are demonic spirits disguised as innocent beings, but they are wolves ready to attack. Don't be afraid. Be on guard. Watch and pray.

Just like there were angels completely surrounding the car that I was in during my dream, God has angels that will protect us every step of the way. We must believe that it's time for us to drive.

Life is not a *do-it-yourself* project. You've been afforded through the blood-bought salvation that Jesus offers you to have the Holy Spirit be your 24/7 heavenly hero. He saved the day for me. I would not have made it without Him. And you can't make it either.

To keep going through the trials and tribulations of this life, you need Jesus and the Holy Spirit. You can't have one without the other, and why would you want to?

Don't act like the children of Israel after they crossed the Red Sea. Remember they had just come out of slavery, where they were forced to make bricks without straw. They were pushed to work long hours and were treated as less than human.

God sent Moses to rescue them, but soon after their deliverance out of slavery, all they did was complain. They didn't know that they wanted freedom. They had become accustomed to the life of slavery, and although they'd prayed for relief, when relief came, they resisted. But freedom was what was offered. It was God's gift to them. God was making good on the promises He'd made to Abraham, and the children of Israel were the beneficiaries of those promises.

Instead, they mumbled and complained constantly. After their great exodus out of Egypt, they held on to the words of Moses that said God would bring them into their promised land. Little did they know that the route to get there was through the wilderness. That place that they found themselves in was a desolate one where there was a lack of food and water. There was no other way for them. It was a part of God's plan.

The promised land felt more like a pit of punishment. They felt abandoned by God. They could not handle the pain of the process. They did not have the opportunity to talk directly to God as we can. They needed Moses to speak for them.

They did not know God as their provider at that point in time. They did not know that He was all they needed until they had no other options. So, because of their complaints, God showered down manna from heaven to prove to them that He would take care of all their needs. He planned for them to go hungry so that through their experience, they would know Him to be their provider.

God caused water to gush out from a rock to quench their thirst. When a need arose, God stepped in to be their answer. He wanted them to rest assured that the essential things of life would always be cared for by Him. God is the source. But that wasn't enough.

Then, to add insult to injury, while Moses retreated to receive the Ten Commandments from God, the children of Israel took all the jewels, gold, silver, and other precious metals that they'd gotten from the Egyptians to create a golden calf to worship. Worshipping God wasn't enough. After all He'd done for them, they felt the need to worship an object instead of the true and living God.

Obviously, their memory was short-circuited. God parted the Red Sea, they walked through on dry land with walls of water on each side of them, He rained down manna from heaven and gave them water out of a rock, and yet they needed to find an object to worship. Does that make sense? Absolutely, it does. It's our adversary, Satan, that works in our thoughts to convince us to leave the sanctuary of our loving God.

The question is why God, the Creator of the universe, would go out of His way to continue to do so many incredible feats for ungrateful people. Love. Love made Him do it, and His character wouldn't allow Him to not keep His promises.

God is still performing marvelous wonders for dissatisfied, disagreeable, and demanding people. This time, the promise comes through Jesus, and it's offered to anyone—no matter your race, creed, or gender, if you accept Jesus as your Savior.

None of the children of Israel who were twenty years of age or older who came out of Egypt mumbling and complaining ever saw the promised land except for two: Joshua and Caleb. They were two of the twelve spies that were sent to spy out the land, but they were the only ones who did not malign the land or their possibility of over-throwing those that lived there. They trusted God and His ability to bring them into a land flowing with milk and honey.

What about you? Do you trust God with your life? Life is hard, and it doesn't discriminate. In light of that, it can be difficult to hold onto a faith in an unseen God when you live in such a cruel world that's full of greed, murders, and robbing-Peter-to-pay-Paul lifestyles. But whether you trust in God or in your ability to pull yourself up by your own bootstraps, life is difficult. Why not try Jesus?

In John 6:48, Jesus said, "I am the bread of life." I didn't know this truth until I was hungry enough. Now I have eternal life. When I needed healing, I ate that bread daily because Jesus said in Matthew 15:26 that healing is the children's bread. It's not the suffering that defines us, but the solution found only in Jesus that creates defining moments.

Life is paved with pain and hardships. It's our privilege to work toward the freedom found on this side of life that is only possible through Jesus. He came to set us free, but it is our choices that ultimately make us free. Stay the course and watch how God shows up just in the nick of time.

12

THE CROSSING

*But when you cross over the Jordan and dwell in
the land which the LORD your God is giving you to
inherit, and He gives you rest from all your enemies
round about, so that you dwell in safety...*

DEUTERONOMY 12:10 NKJV

O ne day, a woman was walking down the street when she spotted
a beggar sitting on the corner. The man was elderly, unshaven,
and ragged. As he sat there, pedestrians walked by him, giving
him dirty looks. They clearly wanted nothing to do with him because
of who he was—a dirty, homeless man. But when she saw him, the
woman was moved to compassion.

It was very cold that day, and the man had his tattered coat—more
like an old suit coat rather than a warm coat—wrapped around him.
She stopped and looked down. "Sir," she asked, "are you alright?"

The man slowly looked up. This was a woman clearly accustomed
to the finer things of life. Her coat was new. She looked like she had
never missed a meal in her life. His first thought was that she wanted
to make fun of him like so many others had done before. "Leave me
alone," he growled.

To his amazement, the woman continued standing. She was smiling—even her white teeth displayed in dazzling rows. "Are you hungry?" she asked.

"No," he answered sarcastically. "I've just come from dining with the president. Now go away."

The woman's smile became even broader. Suddenly the man felt a gentle hand under his arm. "What are you doing, lady?" the man asked angrily. "I said to leave me alone."

Just then a police officer came up. "Is there any problem, Ma'am?" he asked.

"No problem here, Officer," the woman answered. "I'm just trying to get this man to his feet. Will you help me?"

The officer scratched his head. "That's old Jack. He's been a fixture around here for a couple of years. What do you want from him?"

"See that cafeteria over there?" she asked. "I'm going to get him something to eat and get him out of the cold for a while."

"Are you crazy, lady?" the homeless man resisted. "I don't want to go in there!" Then he felt strong hands grab his other arm and lift him up. "Let me go, Officer. I didn't do anything."

"This is a good deal for you, Jack," the officer answered. "Don't blow it."

Finally, and with some difficulty, the woman and the police officer got Jack into the cafeteria and sat him at a table in a remote corner. It was the middle of the morning, so most of the breakfast crowd had already left and the lunch bunch had not yet arrived. The manager strode across the cafeteria and stood by the table. "What's going on here, Officer?" he asked. "What is all this? Is this man in trouble?"

"This lady brought this man in here to be fed," the police officer answered.

"Not in here!" the manager replied angrily. "Having a person like that here is bad for business."

Old Jack smiled a toothless grin. "See, lady. I told you so. Now if you'll let me go. I didn't want to come here in the first place."

The woman turned to the cafeteria manager and smiled. "Sir, are you familiar with Eddy and Associates, the banking firm down the street?"

"Of course, I am," the manager answered impatiently. "They hold their weekly meetings in one of my banquet rooms."

"And do you make a good profit from providing food at the weekly meetings?"

"What business is that of yours?"

"I, sir, am Penelope Eddy, president and CEO of the company."

"Oh."

The woman smiled again. "I thought that might make a difference." She glanced at the cop who was busy stifling a giggle. "Would you like to join us in a cup of coffee and a meal, Officer?"

"No thanks, Ma'am," the officer replied. "I'm on duty."

"Then, perhaps, a cup of coffee to go?"

"Yes, Ma'am. That would be very nice."

The cafeteria manager turned on his heel. "I'll get your coffee for you right away, Officer."

The officer watched him walk away. "You certainly put him in his place," he said.

"That was not my intent. Believe it or not, I have a reason for all this." She sat down at the table across from her amazed dinner guest. She stared at him intently. "Jack, do you remember me?"

Old Jack scanned her face with his old, watery eyes. "I think so—I mean, you do look familiar."

"I'm a little older perhaps," she said. "Maybe I've even filled out more than in my younger days when you worked here, and I came through that very door, cold and hungry."

"Ma'am?" the officer said questioningly. He couldn't believe that such a magnificently turned-out woman could ever have been hungry.

"I was just out of college," the woman began. "I had come to the city looking for a job, but I couldn't find anything. Finally, I was down to my last few cents and had been kicked out of my apartment. I walked the streets for days. It was February, and I was cold and nearly starving. I saw this place and walked in on the off chance that I could get something to eat."

Jack lit up with a smile. "Now I remember," he said. "I was behind the serving counter. You came up and asked me if you could work for something to eat. I said that it was against company policy."

"I know," the woman continued. "Then you made me the biggest roast beef sandwich that I had ever seen, gave me a cup of coffee, and told me to go over to a corner table and enjoy it. I was afraid that you would get into trouble. Then, when I looked over, I saw you put the price of my food in the cash register. I knew then that everything would be all right."

"So, you started your own business?" Old Jack said.

"I got a job that same afternoon. I worked my way up. Eventually, I started my own business that, with the help of God, prospered." She opened her purse and pulled out a business card. "When you are finished here, I want you to pay a visit to Mr. Lyons. He's the personnel director of my company. I'll go talk to him now, and I'm certain he'll find something for you to do around the office." She smiled. "I think he might even find the funds to give you a little advance so that you can buy some clothes and get a place to live until you get on your feet, and if you ever need anything, my door is always open for you."

There were tears in the old man's eyes. "How can I ever thank you?" he said.

"Don't thank me," the woman answered. "Thank Jesus. He led me to you."

Outside the cafeteria, the officer and the woman paused at the entrance before going their separate ways. "Thank you for all your help, Officer," she said.

"On the contrary, Ms. Eddy," he answered. "Thank you. I saw a miracle today, something that I will never forget. And... And thank you for the coffee."

She frowned. "I forgot to ask you whether you used cream or sugar. That's black."

The officer looked at the steaming cup of coffee in his hand. "Yes, I do take cream and sugar—perhaps more sugar than is good for me." He patted his ample stomach.

"I'm sorry," she said.

"I don't need it now," he replied smiling. "I've got the feeling that this coffee you bought me is going to taste as sweet as sugar."[11]

The author of this short story is unknown, but the moral of the story speaks of who we are. Its message is twofold: never judge a person based on the season that they're in, and doing good has an audience: other people and God.

This story makes you feel warm and fuzzy on the inside, right? She did something beautiful, but was it just to free her conscience, or was it because that's just who she was?

---

11. Source unknown.

It's about motivation. Penelope was motivated to help the one that had helped her. When she was down to nothing, he was her hand up. There's nothing wrong with that. In fact, it's a good thing to do.

This is the crossover moment. We're pushing to go from good to great. Our intentions and motivations must tip the scales in the direction of who Jesus is.

What motivates us to perform acts of kindness like this? Are we only charitable toward those that first act amicably with us? Frighteningly, this is true for most of us. It's our human dilemma. It's called reciprocity, and it is especially the religious that are guilty of it.

In this crossing over, it's our number-one job to flip this script on what it means to be a Christian. We must not only change the conversation but how we exist.

Religion has become a dirty word, but it's a new day. Love is our only motivation, and as Shannon Alder once said, "True love is the tide that pulls out to sea, but always returns to kiss the shore at sunrise." The tide has turned, and the time has come for us to rise to do what the Savior did. Love.

What should that look like? It should resemble the attitude of the Good Samaritan that's found in Luke 10:30–37.

The story goes like this:

> A man was going down from Jerusalem to Jericho, and
> he encountered robbers, and they stripped him and beat
> him, and went away leaving him half dead. And by coinci-
> dence a priest was going down on that road, and when he
> saw him, he passed by on the other side. Likewise a Levite
> also, when he came to the place and saw him, passed by
> on the other side. But a Samaritan who was on a journey

came upon him; and when he saw him, he felt compassion, and came to him and bandaged up his wounds, pouring oil and wine on them; and he put him on his own animal, and brought him to an inn and took care of him. On the next day he took out two denarii and gave them to the innkeeper and said, "Take care of him; and whatever more you spend, when I return, I will repay you."

It's important to note here that Jewish religious representatives, both a priest and a Levite, passed by this man and did nothing. In fact, they went out of their way not to come close to him. They moved to the other side of the street to avoid encountering him.

It was a Samaritan that did the heavy lifting. Jews did not associate with Samaritans, although they were related.

Why not? Because they were ethnically a mixed breed and altered many of the Jewish traditions. Therefore, Jews despised them. Yeah, it's those relatives. You know, they're the ones that didn't go to college, they talk loudly, they're boisterous, and they just rub you the wrong way. But hate creates more hate. The Samaritans hated the Jews just as much.

Yeah, it's those relatives. You know, they're the ones that didn't go to college, they talk loudly, they're boisterous, and they just rub you the wrong way.

Yet, it was one of "those relatives," a Samaritan, that interrupted his travels, whether they were for business or pleasure we don't know. He saw a need, and he filled it. He picked up the hurt man, put him on his "ride," took him to a hotel, and nursed him back to health.

When it was time for the Good Samaritan to leave, he made sure that the hotel was paid for so that the man could recuperate. He paid the innkeeper two denarii and promised that whatever the bill was when he returned, he would pay it. At the time, two denarii was worth a lot. It was the equivalent of a laborer's daily wage, according to testamentpress.com.[12]

Can you imagine someone doing this for you? It would change how you show up in the world. Unfortunately, greed is at an all-time high, and most of us are so afraid that someone lying on the side of the road is a fraudster. It's hard to trust that you are really helping someone that's in need.

The point is that we, the Church, need to get off the sidelines and fully engage in the game without fear of the consequences. That means we must know that we're on the same team. We don't compete—we complete what Jesus did.

Our mission has to be driven by Isaiah 61:1–4:

> The Spirit of the Lord GOD is upon me,
> Because the LORD anointed me
> To bring good news to the humble;
> He has sent me to bind up the brokenhearted,
> To proclaim release to captives
>   and freedom to prisoners;
> To proclaim the favorable year of the LORD
>   and the day of vengeance of our God;
> To comfort all who mourn,
> To grant those who mourn in Zion,
> Giving them a garland instead of ashes,

---

12. "Ancient Money Calculator," *Testament Press*, testamentpress.com/ancient-money-calculator.html.

The oil of gladness instead of mourning,
The cloak of praise instead of a disheartened spirit.
So, they will be called oaks of righteousness,
The planting of the LORD, that He may be glorified.
Then they will rebuild the ancient ruins,
 they will raise up the former devastations;
And they will repair the ruined cities,
The desolations of many generations.

Do you remember the wrist bands with WWJD on them? Everyone was wearing them. It stood for What Would Jesus Do. That's my question—what would Jesus do if He were living on earth today?

We know for certain that He would perform miracles, and He is the Master Teacher, but beyond those things—what would He do differently than us?

Would He protest? Would He stand in front of Congress or the Supreme Court holding a sign of protest over abortion? Which side of the argument would He be on? Would He be on the side of the Me Too movement?

What about a prison ministry? Would He do that?

Would He be on YouTube? Would He perform on TikTok? Would He engage in long disputes on X (formerly known as Twitter)? Perhaps, if it drew people to Him.

Would He rent out Carnegie Hall to hold a miracle conference? Or would He work in the local missions as they feed the homeless? Which brings up an enormous problem. How would Jesus handle the epidemic of homelessness?

What would He say about a woman having an abortion? What about attending an LGBTQ-rights rally? Would He be seen at something like that?

Would He go to any church USA and turn over the tables again out of disgust at the "moneychangers" that rob the poor in His name?

I believe He would take worship to the streets. Can you imagine it? Jesus shutting down I-75 with a miracle rally. That would be some kind of sight to see.

I believe He would be most concerned about individuals. He'd hold small-group discussions. After all, He is the living Word.

Jesus's mission hasn't changed. We have. He's still driven to save the lost and sin-sick world.

Now, what about the greater works that Jesus said we would do?

We, the Church, cannot be the salt of the earth as long as we keep sugarcoating the Gospel. We are to be salt and light. Salt makes food tasty, and light gives direction. That's who we are to be.

If we want better, we must give better. Stop waiting on someone else to do what we know needs to be done. It starts with one person. Let it be us.

IN CLOSING

2020 was a defining moment for the world and the Church. We saw COVID-19 rattle the very fabric of our lives and shake everything from its foundation. Weapons now engulf our lives in America. There's fear when we grocery shop, go to the mall, or just drive down the street, and that fear isn't about catching a disease. It's fear of catching a bullet because someone doesn't like what someone said. We don't know who to trust anymore. Members of families are not even safe from each other.

There appears to be a disease of complacency that is prevalent in the world. Heads of state are bullying smaller nations to take hostage their resources, leaving their citizens dead in the streets or on the run for safety. The other nations watch in silence.

God enters with a dream and titles it *Bulletproof*. Only God can take our mess and create a message of hope.

In the mood for blues? We don't have time for that. No pity parties will fix our problems.

After months of hashing over the dream with which I began this book, I found that I'm armed and dangerous, but I'm armed with what? How does that make me dangerous? I am not carrying an

AK-47. I'm armed with the blood of Jesus, the Holy Spirit, prayer, and a resolve to keep going despite the obstacles that chase me down.

This wilderness experience with the Holy Spirit taught me that the biggest losers aren't the gamblers, prostitutes, or homosexuals, as we're taught to believe. He showed me the vulnerable side to their issues, but He also showed me the valuable qualities of those who have chosen to walk those paths—like the art of taking risks, how to go for broke, how to put everything on the line—it's all or nothing. In these qualities—along with their past set of disappointments, letdowns, and broken dreams or promises from people who said they loved them—they ended up in these lifestyles.

These are the ones that He wants to reach. He wants to reset their boundaries—not the qualities He put in them. He just wants to refocus their energies on the right path—for good and not evil.

That's what makes me dangerous. He planted a seed in me that is now a full-grown tree of new life. That tree is becoming ripe with new fruit, and it was watered through prayer. Now let Him plant that seed in you.

When you find your purpose for living, you find the fruit that's necessary to live on. It is a painful process, but the suffering is necessary. Some pills are hard to swallow, but they're the only cure for the disease.

Just as the skillful craftsman chisels away at the wood as he perfectly carves out the violin that will play heavenly string music, so will God perfect all things concerning His Church as He carves out the future that He plans for us. His plan works better than ours.

Today, begin again, trust again, hope again, and love again. No matter what you've been through. Look at your circumstances with new lenses because your possibilities are greater than any failures that you may have experienced. Move to the next chapter of your life because this may be the very thing that unlocks your destiny. Tell your future to get ready.

About the Author

Moments before taking the stage, Lauraine White appears to be a quiet and unassuming woman who is patiently standing on the outside of the spotlight. But as soon as she takes the stage and opens her mouth, her prophetic voice and soulfully melodic sound transcend time and prepare her listeners for worship with her unparalleled love songs devoted to Jesus Christ.

From a place of radical worship, God called Lauraine out of the business and religious world to be a prophetic voice in this season to this generation of seekers. This new season requires God's direction that only comes from HIS prophets. God uses Lauraine's musical abilities to open heavenly portals for those listening to experience new levels in worship, where God shows up and speaks through her. It is a worship experience like no other—God comes into the building, and His glory rests among those engulfed in the "behind-the-veil" experience. Angels' wings are left as evidence of their presence...gold dust is gently dusted on chairs and on the floor as evidence that divine visitations have taken place. Once you go there, it's hard to leave...

How did Lauraine come to be able to usher in such an experience? Through trials by fire! Every test—every trial—brought Lauraine to her knees in prayer, teaching her the art of warfare. God uses Lauraine's musical talents and piercing voice to penetrate the enemies' camps. After this time of testing, God positioned Lauraine to be formally trained and ordained by Apostle Wayne and Dr. Beverly Jackson and by the late Apostle Milton Perry.

Lauraine grew up attending the Church of Christ, where there was no instrumental music and where women did not play *any* role in ministry! But God, in His infinite wisdom, ordered Lauraine's steps, drawing her closer to HIM so that she understands that God created all instruments for His pleasure and that He can use a woman to minister to His people.

It was definitely God's plan to prepare Lauraine through her unique experiences as an entrepreneur, running a successful mortgage company; as a battered wife—one who faced death three times at the hand of her first husband; as one who faced poverty and being ostracized and rejected by those that she thought loved her the most, in order to deliver an extraordinary message—that God wants to be reconciled to His children.

The question is why now and *so* late in her life? When God calls you, it is on HIS time, not yours! It took forty years for Moses to receive his commission to lead the children of Israel out of Egypt. It took seventeen years of preparation before Joseph was delivered from slavery and imprisonment. It took twenty years before Jacob was released from Laban's control. Abraham and Sarah were in their old age when they finally received their promise, Isaac. Lauraine White, at sixty-something, is uniquely positioned to carry this message because nothing else matters.

But Lauraine asks you this question: Is there *anything* too hard for God?

9 798989 634439